Suspended Animation

SUSPENDED ANIMATION

A GIL BECKMAN MYSTERY

W.E. Davis

CROSSWAY BOOKS • WHEATON, ILLINOIS
A DIVISION OF GOOD NEWS PUBLISHERS

Suspended Animation

Published by Crossway Books
a division of Good News Publishers
1300 Crescent Street
Wheaton, Illinois 60187

Cover illustration: Steve Kropp

Cover design: William Paetzold

First printing 1994

Printed in the United States of America

ISBN 0-89107-802-9

The characters and events in this novel are creations of the author's imagination. What likeness they may bear to persons or events, living or dead, past or present, is the likeness of coincidence.

Library of Congress Cataloging-in-Publication Data
Davis, W.E., 1951-
Suspended Animation / W. E. Davis.
p. cm.—(A Gil Beckman mystery)
I. Title. II. Series: Davis, Wally, 1951- Gil Beckman mystery.
PS3554.A93785S86 1994 813'.54—dc20 94-9509
ISBN 0-89107-802-9

02 01 00 99 98 97 96 95 94
15 14 13 12 11 10 9 8 7 6 5 4 3 2 1

To Marcie, my wife
for her support

Barbara Bush, our pastor's wife
for her encouragement and advice

The members of the Pilgrim's
Sunday morning Bible study class
of Grace Community Church
Lake Forest, California
for keeping my feet on the ground
and my head out of the clouds.

ONE

The sheriff charged across the open town square, his six-gun blazing as outlaw bullets kicked dirt up around his feet. He dove over the water trough and shouted at his assailants, "Give it up! You'll never get away with this!"

"Oh, yeah?" yelled the leader of the outlaw gang punctuating his comeback with a volley of lead.

The sheriff looked at the reflection in a nearby store window and spotted a man on a roof across the street drawing a bead on him. The lawman rolled quickly and fired once without taking aim. The outlaw stood, frozen in place, then his rifle slipped from his grasp, and he slowly toppled over the edge of the roof, landing with a thud on the ground below, out of sight behind a wagon.

"One down!" the sheriff shouted.

"There's still three of us left, and we're all better than Slim!" the outlaw leader called back.

"We'll see about that!" The sheriff crawled from the trough to a nearby wagon while the bandits emptied their guns in his direction.

"Ha! Ya missed!" the unscathed sheriff taunted. He waited until two of the outlaws stuck their heads up for a peek and fired two quick rounds, dispatching both of them. They staggered out from their hiding places and dropped dramatically in the middle of the square.

"Now it's your turn, Blackie!" the sheriff declared.

"No, wait. I give up!" Blackie threw his gun out. "I'm comin' out! Don't shoot!"

Blackie emerged cautiously from the shadows of the alley with his hands held high above him. As he walked cautiously out into the open his eyes shifted nervously from side to side.

The sheriff eased out slowly from under the wagon. Keeping his gun trained on Blackie, he moved toward the outlaw. They met in the center of the square, near the villain's fallen comrades. A crowd of onlookers pressed in, unafraid, to surround the two remaining combatants.

Their eyes locked in silent warfare. The sheriff raised an eyebrow, but when a noise in the crowd caused him to flick his gaze away briefly, Blackie made his move dropping his arms and kicking the gun out of his opponent's hand.

Once again on equal ground, the two men circled each other warily. Blackie took the initiative and threw the first blow, hitting the sheriff hard enough to make the lawman's head jerk sharply to the side.

But the sheriff recovered quickly and blocked Blackie's second punch, then retaliated with a solid blow to the body. Blackie doubled over and the lawman gave him a knee in the face, standing the dazed outlaw back up straight. Rearing back, the sheriff delivered a final blow to his opponent's jaw, and the outlaw dropped unconscious to the dirt, his arms and legs spread-eagle.

The onlookers broke out into a smattering of applause then quickly drifted away in all directions while the sheriff, Blackie, and the other three gunmen picked themselves up, dusted themselves off, and then wandered away together as if they were old friends, chattering and laughing and critiquing their performance.

I watched the scene unfold with passive disinterest, having

seen it innumerable times before. Oh, sometimes Blackie won, but basically it was the same every hour.

Leaning back on the weathered wood bench, I stared out over the sagging rooftops of the western ghost town. A deserted barrel house stood a few yards from the cemetery, a regular "boot hill" with several "hand-chiseled" concrete tombstones but mostly wind-smoothed wooden crosses with painted epitaphs that were no longer readable.

The doors of the saloon across the street flapped in the breeze, and I could almost hear the long-gone cancan dancers yelping with feigned delight as they strutted for the drunken patrons. I smiled a bit to myself as I pictured Dolly high-kicking in her fishnet stockings. What a gal!

It was seven at night and the declining sun cast a pinkish-orange glow that backlit the ancient buildings. The few clouds that hovered in the distance were blue, and the contrast with the dusk sky was striking.

I surveyed the scene as oblivious to the throngs of noisy, swarming people as they were to me. They were also much too busy to notice—much less appreciate—the display being presented for them in the sky above. The masses were consumed with the rides, shows, junk food, and trinkets with which they assaulted themselves. After all, they paid over twenty dollars each for admission to this amusement park, and, by golly, they were going to be amused.

Slowly I stood, giving my forty-year-old muscles a chance to stretch without pain. I glanced at my watch and urged it to speed up. In a couple of hours the park would close for the day and peaceful, blessed silence would once again settle like a heavy fog, making the whole theme park truly a ghost town.

I enjoyed the park then. No people to bother me, no whining kids crying for more junk, no tired moms and dads spending way too much for sugared goodies or mediocre burgers and those ubiquitous gotta-have-it toys destined for instant relegation to toy box dungeons. There would be blessed, eerie silence.

All the atmosphere present in the ghost town became real and effective after the paying customers piled into their cars and headed home. Some of the buildings were actual, transplanted western American edifices discovered in some long-forgotten Arizona town and disassembled, then moved here and put back together board-by-board. Others were "new," built to look as if they were old. The sad part was that few could tell the difference, and no one cared.

To think that man could imitate the ravages of years of weather upon a structure was remarkable, yet sad, as it devalued the real thing.

That bothered me, I admit. I love the Old West, and marveled at the hundred-year-old structures I had seen in some of the ghost towns I'd visited over the years: Virginia City, Nevada; Elkhorn, Montana; Silver City, Idaho; but especially Bodie, California, probably the best preserved ghost town in existence. The feeling one gets strolling on the same ground and up the same wooden steps that our forebears walked upon takes you back to a simpler, albeit harder, time, when the pace of life was slower, the work tougher, and the virtues and their contrary vices more clearly distinguishable.

Except for the asphalt underfoot, this ghost town I now meandered through gave me pretty much the same feeling, only the knowledge that it wasn't real kept that feeling from lingering. Nevertheless, it was a creepy but interesting place at night.

And not just the ghost town. The theme rides like Space Race, Solomon's Mine, and The Time Machine, each decorated with dioramas and animated figures, were designed to take the riders into another time and place, to make them forget the problems of their lives for a spell. But it didn't quite work when the park was open. There was always some kid crying or throwing his snow cone on you; or some loud, obnoxious jerk intentionally splashing you in the wet rides at all the wrong times; or foreigners talking too loud in an unidentifiable tongue that disrupted the mood. And you had to sit in metal buckets that twisted and tilted down an endless track listening to prerecorded narration that was scratchy and barely audible. Other than that, it was pretty effective.

At night, though, that was the time. With no distractions you could easily walk through the scenes with just a flashlight and transport yourself wherever and whenever you wanted. And you weren't restricted to sitting in a cart-on-a-conveyor, traveling much too fast to take it all in.

This is the time I liked. If you have to be a security guard, it might as well be here, and at night. I'm a retired police officer-turned-security guard . . . Well, okay, I didn't retire, I just quit. A little burned out, I had wanted to start my own business, so I withdrew my money from the state retirement fund and pulled the pin on law enforcement. Almost. I realized quickly that I needed a medical plan now that I was about ready to admit I was aging. But I couldn't afford one on my own, so I signed on as a security guard at the amusement park where they offered an adquate benefit package. Naturally they promised quick promotions for a man of my experience, and naturally I believed them.

I know what you're thinking, and you're right, it was a stupid move. To be honest with you, I didn't check with God before I made it. But I'm not telling you all this to get your opinion, just to give you some background on me, to explain why I was there that night.

This park wasn't a carnival. It was, and still is, one of the country's largest theme parks—although not that well known outside the state—and it takes in hundreds of thousands of dollars every day. Even so, for a sworn, commissioned police officer to become a security guard—voluntarily, no less—is a definite tumble down the status ladder. Most cops think of security guards as rent-a-cops who can't get hired by a real law enforcement agency but still want to play the game. A real cop would sooner bite the barrel than stoop to that level. That's just false pride, of course, because security guards are as necessary in this country as cops, and good people are always sought after. Security guards don't enjoy the same respect in the public's view, however, and certainly have little of the authority that cops wield. To most cops, becoming a security guard would be a bitter pill to swallow.

I wasn't in a position to be proud. I took the job and went to work. I liked nights for the solitude it afforded in addition to being free during the day to run my business. Not that there was much to do. I didn't have enough money to keep the business going full-bore.

In fact, it had all but died on the vine. A year after I started it, the thing petered out. Lack of operating capital. It was a mail order business featuring gift items for cops. The venture started with a bang, but I soon realized I had to keep the advertisements going to secure customers, and that was eating up all my revenue. You have to have money to make money. Soon—much sooner than I ever anticipated—I had to stop advertising altogether, and, in the mail order business, you don't get any orders without ads.

So here I was. The P.D. wasn't in any mood to hire me back—the city manager had a no re-hire policy—so desperation drove me to the park. I knew a few folks, ex-cops, and getting hired was relatively simple. They put me on graveyard to learn the layout of the place, and I liked the solitude so much I stayed on nights once I realized that a promised promotion and pay raise were no more than empty words, the grand rhetoric of someone without the authority or desire to carry them out. Plus, being seen working here as a security guard embarrassed me more than I cared admitting. A little quirk in my personality called pride that God was still working on.

At night I made the rounds of the park in the khaki shirt and dark brown trousers of the security guard wearing a police style Sam Browne belt with everything but the gun, making sure no kids had sneaked in, opening doors for custodians, opening doors for mechanics, opening doors for painters, opening doors for plumbers . . . .

Theft is a problem even in a fantasy land, and custodians

and other maintenance workers weren't allowed to have keys. Some supervisors had keys to their area, or to certain doors, but only security people had a full set of master keys. When I wasn't shagging doors for someone else, and when time permitted, I used my keys to enter the indoor rides—dark rides, we called them—and scout around.

Trekking about the indoor rides, although permitted, wasn't really encouraged. Time frequently didn't allow it, either. But I got to where I could anticipate who would be calling at what time to have which door opened, so I could get there ahead of him and have time to do what I really enjoyed: prowling around the interior of the attractions.

This night was no different; at least it started the same as all the others. I opened the House of Tacos in Spanish City for a custodian, locked him in, and knew I had an hour before anybody else would need me. As I made my way to Solomon's Mine, I took careful note of my surroundings. It wasn't unusual to be followed by Javier Jaime Brito, my sergeant.

He was a likable enough guy, good-natured off duty, laughed easily most of the time, but took his work a little too seriously to the point of worry—not healthy concern and professionalism, but unnecessary fretting. In fact, he was downright distracting and a bit too picky. Only twenty-one himself, he assumed all his subordinates were either incompetent or lazy, and he acted accordingly, having a tendency to oversupervise, be too harsh and judgmental, and make hasty, sometimes rash, decisions. From where I stood, I attributed Sergeant Brito's actions to a lack of experience, both on the job and in life in general, coupled with an intense desire to prove himself and advance in the company without any real self-confidence to back it up.

That his name sounded like burrito was not lost on any of us, and pronouncing it that way had become the norm. He got a little upset at first, but settled down when he realized it wasn't going to do any good. I suspect that he had been forced to deal with that all his life. Truth is, he looked like a macho combo burrito. In fact, he went by his middle name, Jaime, because when he was in grade school (in New Mexico, where he was born) the kids called little Javier Brito "Heavier Burrito." He admitted that to me once during a moment of weakness at three in the morning when he was too sleepy to restrain himself.

Life can be very funny at times all by itself.

Brito was one of those guys who built his empire on the carcasses of his fellow workers by constantly trying to find something wrong with the way they did their job even if there was nothing wrong to find. I'd seen that type of supervisor before at the P.D. all too many times. As a result, I kept a wary eye out as I made my rounds.

But my experience as a street cop hadn't been wasted. Many times I snuck up behind Brito—who thought he was watching me—and startled him. Once I saw him lumbering up a pathway through Camp Wilderness so sleepy that his eyes were almost closed. I drove my electric cart toward him to see if he wanted a ride. He kept walking, and I quickly realized he was oblivious to me. He finally heard me at the last second, but his mind was so slow on the uptake because of his need for sleep that he didn't know what it was behind him. He was so surprised that he jumped around quickly and tried to karate chop my electric cart! When he saw it was me and realized that he should have noticed me long before I got so close, he stammered through a lame excuse and lumbered off to find a less experienced quarry, leaving me doubled in laughter.

As I approached the mine ride on this warm, clear night, I took a short, but somewhat serpentine, route through the park, stopping at the rear door of Solomon's Mine. I stood still in the dark listening, making sure I was alone. In the distance I could hear a police siren somewhere on the city streets well outside the park. A light, warm breeze rustled some shrubs nearby, but all else was quiet. Confident that I hadn't been followed, I looked around one final time, slid my master key into the lock, eased the knob, and went in.

The door opened into the shop where the cars and animated figures were taken for repair. It was cold and smelled of mildew and grease. Tools were scattered on workbenches and chairs amidst disembodied heads and small flanged wheels from the carts in which the guests sat. Metal lockers with personal photos and pinup posters taped to the doors lined the wall opposite the workbench, and a break room was nearby, empty except for a square table and chairs and a small refrigerator. There were several empty candy wrappers on the table and a half-empty paper coffee cup. Or perhaps it was half-full, depending upon your outlook on life.

I walked down a short hall past a dirty rest room, ducked around a corner, and went up several steps through a dark, narrow tunnel with gunite walls, the concrete-based material sprayed onto a metal framework to simulate granite. It was fairly effective, especially in the near-dark of the ride, but the underside was a mass of steel beams, two-by-fours, and heavy wire mesh.

I found myself on the edge of a rock looking down into the main cavern of the mine. I slowly moved the beam of my high intensity, Krypton-bulbed cop flashlight over the scene below me. All the workers in their Egyptian-looking skirts and straight black hair stood poised with their tools in mid-swing, waiting for someone to throw the switch that would start them working again for the amusement of the ungrateful masses.

"Hmmmm," I mused aloud. I noted the distinct absence of any people dressed or looking like Hebrews. After all, this was Solomon's mine, the great King over all of Israel (for you Bible history buffs, it had not yet been divided into two kingdoms), and not the property of some Egyptian pharaoh. Oh well, whoever the person was in the park's Design and Planning department that planned and designed this ride probably was a wet-behind-the-ears college grad with a lot of grand ideas and no real knowledge to back it up. Historical accuracy is usually not an essential element of theme park rides. Entertainment is the key, just like books, movies, and television.

That reminds me of a court case I was once involved in. It was a civil suit. The family of a dead guy—a convicted felon who was shot by a cop while committing an armed robbery and was aiming his gun at police officers—sued for wrongful death. The jury—God love 'em—found in the bad guy's favor because they thought the cop should have shot the gun out of his hand instead of killing him. Too much bad T.V. for those people. They ignored the reality that it's impossible to do that in real life, not to mention highly unsafe. But that's what they've seen portrayed for years on the screen, so it must be true. John Wayne did it, so why couldn't the cop?

I returned through the opening—called a sneak-in—and went down into the work area. There were many sneak-ins like this into the ride from the shop areas, which employees referred to as *backstage*, the part of the ride the public saw being the *stage*. The whole idea of the park is that of a play, a show. These sneak-ins were all but invisible to the public. For one thing, these rides are usually more dark than light, and the sneak-ins are designed so people would have to turn around in their seats and look backwards to notice them. In the mine the doorways resembled short tunnels that disappeared around a bend or had a black curtain hanging over them to block light from the backstage filtering into the ride. And since the rides went too fast to barely get a good look at the action itself, why spend any time trying to see the employee entrances?

Because the rides went fast and the lights were so dim, it was also unnoticeable to the passing guests just how decrepit the scenery and animated figures were. Up close, under the scrutiny of a flashlight, I could see the poor detail of the characters: wing tips on the mine foreman; excess glue around the eyeball of a man pushing an ore cart; tacky, dusty clothing; old Beatle wigs on just about everyone. Just as in real life, what looks so good from a distance turns out to be mostly junk once you get close enough to inspect it. The whole scene reminded me of 1 Corinthians 13—all sounding brass and tinkling cymbal.

As seen in the distance through a tunnel in the mountain, the gleaming pyramid that was supposed to be far off in the desert turned out to be a foot high and covered with glitter. The tunnel was nothing more than a backlit crevice. Illusion. It was all illusion.

As I turned to go back through the sneak-in I saw something on the ground and put my light on it. It was a park employee name tag. Stooping to pick it up, I noticed the pins on the back had been bent, as though it had been stepped on. The name on the front was Everett. I slipped it into my pocket. I could turn it in to dispatch later.

I ducked back into the shop area and turned to look at the underside of the mountain. A maze of steel beams, wire mesh, and gray gunite distorted the image I had of the other side. I went down a short flight of stairs and into another opening nearby and found myself seemingly many miles away and on a different level. I stepped over the track that guides the guest carts and stood in the middle of the main mine shaft. It looked considerably smaller here than it did from above but was substantial nonetheless with hundreds of mechanical people. There were even static, non-moving people, and many aspects of life in those days (as the designers imagined it, at least) were crammed into a small space. It was much like a model railroad setup where everything is condensed into a smaller than scale space: the Mississippi River flows from the Statue of Liberty to the Grand Canyon in an area four feet-by-eight feet.

Daily events that wouldn't occur in a mine were depicted here, including a wedding and a funeral, just to give the feeling of life in Solomon's day. I went from figure to figure looking for authentic detail that wasn't there.

The hour was about up, and I knew I would be needed outside, so I started making my way to one of the sneak-ins. As my flashlight beam passed over a group of figures, something caught my eye. I'm not sure what it was that made me hesitate. You know how it works. You're looking at something that looks fine, but you have this uneasy feeling about it. Then finally you realize that there's nothing wrong with it; it's just that it doesn't belong where it is.

One of the figures in this group gave me that feeling. It had a different quality than the others. It looked more . . . alive!

It wasn't. Dressed up in one of the costumes worn by the Egyptian workers was a young man—not a mannequin, or mechanical figure—a real person in a state of suspended animation.

In other words, he was dead.

Two

At first I was surprised, perhaps even shocked. Adrenaline began to pump through my system giving me the shakes—not from fear, but in preparation for action. I shined my light around the man-made cavern making sure I was alone, although it was just a reflex, a precaution, as my instinct told me this boy had been dead for awhile already. This was an amusement park, for goodness sake! Why—and how—did this happen here?

Positive the killer, or killers, had long since departed, I turned my attention back to the deceased. He was seated in a chair that matched those in the break room, his eyes staring blankly straight ahead, head cocked to one side, arms hanging limply by his side. His legs were spread and his tennis shoed feet turned awkwardly at angles that would have been uncomfortable for a conscious person. I knew immediately that he had been placed there probably after his death, by hasty people unconcerned with his comfort. I checked the body closely without touching it, except to confirm by the lack of a pulse what I already knew. I also noticed a small amount of blood around the base of the neck. It had trickled down from some type of wound higher up on the head. I lifted the hair of the black wig that had been haphazardly perched on his head and saw matted blood on the back of his cranium. Closer inspection revealed the unmistakable evidence of blunt trauma, the details of which I'll spare you except to say that his skull in this area had been crushed by a heavy object.

Rigor mortis had not yet set in except in his eyelids. It always starts in the smaller muscles. That placed time of death in the less than four-to-five hour range, give or take. He was still warm to the touch, so make that three-to-four hours. There was abundant post-mortem lividity in his lower legs and hands, the extremities that were hanging down and served as collectors for the blood which, now that the heart no longer kept it flowing, had settled by gravity into the lowest parts of his body. I pressed my finger against his ankle and let up. His skin blanched but returned to deep purple like the surrounding tissue when I released pressure, indicating that the blood had not yet clotted. Still in the four-hour range since death. Too close for comfort.

He wasn't a pretty sight, but I'd seen worse. There wasn't much blood on the ground, but that alone didn't mean he wasn't killed where he sat. I'd seen wounds like this before, and maybe a quarter cup of blood would leak out. The rest of the bleeding was internal. But the lack of other signs and the way he was dressed up made me think he was clubbed at another location and brought here. As to precisely how long ago that had been, I'd leave that calculation to the coroner.

An involuntary shudder ran up my back and jerked my shoulders, and a prayer—more like a questioning plea—passed from my lips.

"Dear God, what has been done here?"

Even as I said it, an answer of sorts came into my mind, whether from God or just from my own will, I don't know. But the message was plain. I had to find out what had happened.

I glanced around for the weapon but quickly realized there were too many possibilities for me to find it in a few seconds. There were large rocks, mining tools . . . Shoot, the place was full of murder weapons. I'd have to let the cops find it.

I didn't recognize him as an employee of the park, but there were over fourteen hundred of them, and I hadn't met them all. I started to pick up my radio to call the incident in, then thought better of it. Dispatch might not be able to hear me from deep inside the mountain. And the killer could be an employee who might still be around, maybe even have a radio. Most of the graveyard shift carried them.

I needed a little time. This poor guy wasn't going anywhere. The local cops would cordon off the area as soon as they got here to start the investigation, and I wouldn't be able to look around freely then. Five, ten minutes would be enough for what I wanted to do.

Taking out my note pad, I quickly sketched the position of the body and checked the ground surrounding it for footprints. There were several, including mine. None were really distinguishable. A set of work boots, common for this area. Tennis shoes. Those looked like they could be the victim's.

I noticed another shoe print some distance away. It appeared different from the others. I squatted down to get a better look. Working my flashlight from all angles I could tell the print was that of a dress shoe: flat, smooth sole, possibly leather, narrow toe, rubber heel, no noticeable wear. None of the employees who worked in here wore dress shoes as a rule. Because of the machinery and heavy objects they dealt with, the maintenance people were required to wear those tasteless, yet functional, steel-toed jobs. The ride operators usually wore black leather tennis shoes, and although they weren't supposed to be in here, they frequently violated the rules and took shortcuts. Then there was always the possibility of a supervisor coming in to check something, or even a department head.

But why here on this particular night? In my mind this shoe print didn't belong. I drew a quick sketch of it in my notebook and compared it to my shoe. Even with a European pointed toe it was still a little shorter than my size elevens. Maybe a nine or so, no unusual wear patterns, no defects, a clean, sharp print . . . . possibly a new shoe. The cops would photograph it if no one stepped on it first, but I wanted it for myself.

After looking around in the immediate vicinity for a few minutes and not seeing anything else, I went outside to report in, checking carefully for . . . well, for anyone who might see me coming out. I locked the door quietly behind me. Pulling my radio out of the leather pouch, I moved it up to my mouth, but before I could key the mike and say anything the radio coughed and the dispatcher called me. She sounded irritated.

"Unit one-thirty-one, please acknowledge!"

"Unit one-thirty-one here. Go ahead." I tried to sound nonchalant, like I'd been there all the time just waiting for her to call. By the tone of her voice, though, I knew she had been trying to call for some time and I wasn't answering. That's one of the reasons we're not supposed to go into the rides for any length of time.

Someone else probably had to do my rounds for a while, and Brito was presumably out looking for me, hoping to find me sleeping. I figured Jaime was being especially conscientious, thinking that burning someone like me—a former career cop and homicide detective—would surely give his career an upward boost.

Well, I thought, sorry to disappoint you. Better luck next time.

"Unit one-thirty-one, return to the station. Sergeant Brito wants to talk to you." They had tried using police radio codes once, but too many of the guards had trouble understanding. There was too much turnover of personnel, and the brass here at the park didn't want to learn the codes in order to eavesdrop, so they went back to plain English.

"Negative," I said, using one of the few radioese terms left. "Call me at the entrance to the mine ride." I couldn't leave the crime scene, besides, I didn't really want to waste my time talking to Brito anyway.

The phone in the call box at the ride entrance rang immediately. I picked it up and started talking before she could say anything.

"Listen, we've got a problem."

"No, *you* got a problem, Officer Beckman!" replied an angry Sergeant Brito.

So he wasn't out looking for me after all. He was in the office.

"Where have you been sleeping for the past hour?" he growled.

"Nowhere," I said. "I've been in the mine and you'll never guess what I found." I paused for a second to let him guess, but there was only a stony silence, so I continued. "We've got ourselves a dead kid. Murdered." I stopped again to let that sink in.

"Don't fool around, Gil. What were you doing in there, catching a nap? You probably had a dream."

He didn't believe me!

"I'm not one of the boneheads you're used to dealing with here, Jaime." I have an annoying tendency sometimes to be rather ungracious when referring to people less fortunate than myself. "I was walking around in the mine and I found a dead kid. Call the P.D."

"*What?* Is this another one of your stupid jokes?"

"No, Jaime. Guaranteed. I really mean it."

"Okay, I'll be right out to take a look. It better be true." He hung up.

I looked at the phone receiver with an *I don't believe this guy* look on my face. He's going to come out and take a look, like I don't recognize a dead body when I see one? I called the dispatcher back.

"Dispatch."

"Wendy, it's me again. Gil. Did Jaime phone the P.D. or tell you to do it?"

"What for?"

"He didn't say anything?"

"No, he just got up and left, muttering. Why?"

"Call the P.D., would you? There's a dead kid in the mine ride. He was murdered."

"Oh, my gosh, Gil, Are you sure?"

Wendy was a good egg and I knew she wasn't really questioning my powers of observation. She just had trouble believing it.

"I'll tell you about it later, Wendy. Just call them, okay? Then call the receiving gate guard to let them know . . . No, wait. Don't tell anyone else just yet. The cops will fly right by the gate guard anyway. Talk to you later. Here comes Jaime. I can see him running through the ghost town. Never saw him move so fast!" I laughed. "Thanks. Bye."

As I hung up I could imagine her sitting there with her mouth open, but I knew she'd do what I told her. She wanted to get a job with the P.D. and figured I'd make a good reference. Wendy was a cute, little, natural blonde, giving credence to none of the dumb-blonde jokes, and would do well in a P.D. communications center. I hoped she got hired soon.

I heard a noise and saw Brito lumbering up the path, his shirt soaked with sweat.

"Over here, Sarge." I waved for him to meet me on the loading dock. He was out of breath when he got there so I did all the talking. "I know you don't believe this, so I'm going to show you, but I want you to be careful not to contaminate the crime scene. Let's go in this way."

I motioned toward the tunnel entrance where the guests in their carts first enter the ride. "You'll be able to see it from the track just fine." To my surprise he followed without hesitation. His only comment, besides grumbling and heavy breathing, was to mumble again that I had better be telling the truth.

I led the way into the tunnel, careful not to step on the rails. They were treacherous because of the grease on them and several guards in the past had injured themselves trying to walk on top. Beginners.

We followed the cart track around several bends, then the

wall to the right gave way to a large cavern. We were overlooking the main mine which was also dark except for our high-intensity flashlights. Brito's light hit the kid.

"Are you sure that's a person?" Brito asked.

"Former person."

Brito moved his light about and peered closer.

"Holy cow! You weren't kidding!

"I knew that," I said.

"We better call the cops!"

"I had Wendy do it already. They'll be here any second now. I'll wait outside to guide them in. Besides, they'll want to talk to me. You should go back to the station and notify the chief." I hadn't realized at the time that I was giving my supervisor orders. It just came out so naturally. Apparently he didn't notice either because he immediately turned and trotted off mumbling. He had no experience at this and was probably a little rattled. Besides, a murder under his nose would not help his career advancement possibilities much.

The police arrived a few minutes later and started doing their thing while I watched. As they went through their paces I felt a twinge of regret for having left the police department, especially since some of the cops were treating me like just another security guard. It's hard to be outside the circle after so many years on the inside. And with cops, the circle is usually a closed one.

I was interviewed by Officer Meyer, a rookie who didn't know me and wasn't interested in my theories. He was a young guy, tall, skinny, marine haircut, who didn't deviate from his academy-taught list of questions. I could almost hear Joe Friday saying, "Just the facts."

"What's your name, sir?"

"Gil Beckman."

"Gilbert?"

I cringed. "Yeah."

"Middle name?"

"None."

"And your position here at the park?"

I paused, looked down at my clearly marked brown and khaki uniform, then looked back up at Officer Meyer. "Security officer."

"Security guard," he said slowly, writing it down without looking up.

"Security *officer*," I repeated with emphasis.

"Yes sir," he said, but didn't correct his notes. "What time did you find the deceased?"

I told him the approximate time and he pressed me to be exact.

I shrugged. "That's it, give or take a few minutes. I didn't look at my watch."

"Okay. Tell me what you saw."

I gave him a brief synopsis, not bothering to mention why I was in the mine, and he wrote hurriedly, not looking up from the paper. When I told him I thought the kid was already dead when placed in the chair, he didn't write it down but smiled patronizingly and said to leave the theories to the professionals. At that I pretty much clammed up, only giving him what he asked for, deciding I'd wait to talk to the detectives.

Finally, the homicide dick arrived. I was standing in a dark corner outside the mine watching the beehive of activity when a familiar figure strolled up, his long legs stepping smoothly and both hands thrust deep into the pockets of his unnecessary trench coat. The red glow of a cigarette cast a strange, eerie light onto his face, and I recognized him immediately. Theo Brown, my former partner. I hadn't seen him for over a year, and he never returned my calls.

He stopped and conferred with Officer Meyer who pointed toward me. Theo looked my way and stared as Meyer hit me in the face with the beam of one of those retina-burning cop flashlights. Even after he turned it off, I was blind, long enough for Theo to move beside me unseen.

"Well, well," he said. "Fancy meeting you here, Gil."

"Good to see you too, Theo," I said, looking toward the

sound of his voice but seeing only white spots. "And I mean that figuratively. If he does that again I'm going to break his flashlight."

Theo ignored my threat and moved right into a perfunctory line of questioning, disregarding that he had been my partner for years and hadn't seen me for awhile. "Meyer tells me you found the body."

I nodded.

"So, what do you think? You got a line on anything yet?"

I shook my head slowly as I tried to focus on Theo's face as my vision returned. "Not a thing."

"He told me what you said, hardly seems like that's all you know."

"It's all he wanted to learn."

Theo rolled his eyes. "We're inundated with rookies. This guy doesn't know who you are. So what do you know that you didn't tell him?"

I gave him everything, including my sketch of the shoe print, and told him what I thought about the kid being placed in the chair.

"Was he killed here, do you think?" he asked, taking a final draw on his smoke then dropping the butt and stepping on it.

"Had to be. No way someone could carry in a body and dump it in there without attracting notice."

"How long do you think he's been there?" Theo lit another.

"Those'll kill you," I said.

"I tried stopping; you know that. It almost killed me."

"I don't know how long he's been there," I said, returning to the question. "The park closed at nine, but this ride was down all day for periodic repair. You'll have to check with ride maintenance to find out what time the last employee left, but it was probably around five. Dayshift handled that chore today, I believe. You guys got a line on who he is?"

"I was hoping you'd know."

"Not offhand, but I found this inside." Out of my pocket

I pulled the name tag I had found. It was green. Employees in this area wore blue name tags. I handed it to Brown and chuckled to myself at the irony. Even in the midst of horror I usually found something to laugh about. It's what kept me sane.

"What's this?" Brown asked.

"I found it in the ride just before I found the body. It might be his."

"What makes you think so?"

"Not the kind they wear in this area. We can check it."

"Go ahead." He handed it back to me. "I'll talk to you some more later." He turned and Officer Meyer escorted him into the ride.

Determined not to let Theo's somewhat cold reception bother me, I got right down to the business at hand. I phoned dispatch from a nearby call box, which was cleverly disguised as the kneecap of an Egyptian pharaoh or something. How many Everett's could there be here? Through the park computer Wendy obtained a full profile on the name on the tag. The physical description matched the victim. He was an eighteen-year-old college student who worked as a ride operator in the Flapper Zone, a pre-depression themed area, known to employees as the Boring Twenties.

His name didn't ring a bell with me. Everett Curran. Who was this kid that made him important enough for someone to kill? This wasn't a crime of passion or the result of a robbery gone wrong. At least it didn't look like one. This had the smell of a hit—a murder of purpose. It was bizarre and cried out for a motive. Somebody went to a lot of trouble to dress this kid up. A drug deal? Maybe. Could a kid named Everett do drugs?

As I thought about it two familiar figures strode quickly into the area. One was the security chief, Harry Clark, a short, overweight, balding, nearsighted man. He had a pleasant, almost jovial personality, but, in general, was not to be trusted. If you were his neighbor, you'd love him. It was quite different being his employee.

Harry had been a lieutenant with a neighboring P.D., and all I knew about him prior to coming here to work for him was that he was always smiling and seemed harmless, nearly ineffectual. The problem, I was told by some of my friends who worked under him, was the hand that wasn't patting you on the back was getting ready to plunge a knife into it. Harry was a company man and cared for his employees only so long as they didn't go at odds with the company, be it P.D. or amusement park.

To be fair to him, Harry had hired me and I appreciated it. Although he had expressed doubts about my judgment for having left the department as I had—and who didn't?—he said he was glad to have someone of my experience on board. He said he needed a good administrative sergeant to coordinate training and operations. That was two years ago and here I still was, a graveyard door-shaker. Oh well, it was my own fault, I suppose. I believed him.

Harry looked a little bleary-eyed at this early hour and his clothes were rumpled: cheap corduroy jacket; white shirt; brown cotton pants; heavy, thick-soled tan suede shoes; and the end of his skinny tie a good five, six inches above his belt. In fact, with his rosy cheeks and nervous smile, he would have made a good hairless Santa.

In contrast to Harry was the spiffy appearance of the man next to him, his boss Senior Vice President John Hayes. Hayes was a strange-looking duck with red, slicked-down hair, freckles, a pasty pallor on his face and hands, and no command presence whatsoever. He did not strike me as being overly intelligent, which was borne out by his business decisions—the general state of the park was his responsibility. At least it was supposed to work that way. When things were good, he took the credit; when they were bad, subordinates got fired. He wore expensive clothes, traditional round-toed wing tips, and carried grudges, to which all five of his ex-wives could attest.

What Hayes lacked in physical stature he made up for in power. The president was just a figurehead, a cheerleader for the semiannual employee rallies and newspaper photo opportunities, and the owners gave Hayes virtual free-rein over the park, rarely overruling his decisions. Although I tried to find something about him to like, I found very little. But I'm that way with authority figures I guess, right or wrong. I'm just wary about people to whom God has given authority who don't acknowledge Him in return. What's that old saying about power and corruption?

When a serious incident like this happens you can count on the big shots showing up, usually so they can see what they can do to hush things up. Things like this can have a negative impact on attendance, although I knew in this case attendance might even go up because of the curiosity seekers that would want to see where the kid was snuffed.

Hayes would probably want to raise admission prices because they had a new attraction.

Harry saw me and walked over to where I was standing. He shook my hand, congratulated me for finding the body, then introduced me to John Hayes.

"We've met," said Hayes casually as he shook my hand. I nodded and smiled through clenched teeth. He had one of those annoying handshakes that reminded you of a dead trout—limp, soft, and unfeeling. "How did you happen to find him?" Hayes asked.

I shrugged. "Just going through the ride and I stumbled onto him. Quite accidental." He nodded then turned away from me without further comment. Harry followed him like a puppy.

They made their way to the ride entrance. As expected, they tried to walk right into the middle of goings-on, but a salty, uniformed old dog with twenty-plus years as a cop, all of them in patrol, stepped in front of them. They protested, throwing out their names and titles, but the veteran cop didn't budge.

"I don't care if you're Prince Charles and Lady Di," Salty said. "This ride is a crime scene, it belongs to me right now, and you can't go in there. If my chief walks up with the president of the U.S. of A., they'll stand out here with you. No one's gonna traipse through my evidence. If you'll be so kind as to stay put, I'll have the Lieutenant come over and talk to you."

"I want your name and badge number," Hayes demanded, shaking his finger at the cop. The officer reached into his shirt pocket without taking his eyes off Hayes and handed a card to him.

"My pleasure," Salty said. "You can write out your complaint on the back while you're waitin' out here."

They retreated scowling, vengeance in their eyes. I smiled. *That's one for the cops.* I knew there would be no complaint. Hayes had enough trouble with a death on park property, not to mention it being a murder. And Harry, an ex-cop himself, knew from his years on the force that the cop was right. Only certain people can enter a crime scene.

The officer who was responsible for writing the initial report was finished with me, and I had learned all I was going to here. I checked with Lt. Brown then slipped out quietly and headed for the employee cafeteria to get a cup of coffee.

At this time of night all that was available was junk food from vending machines and free coffee. I wasn't hungry; I just wanted to think. My shift would be over soon, and my involvement in this had pretty much excluded me from my normal duties. I drew a cup and took a sip. It tasted burnt, just like the coffee at church between services.

I didn't care. I was used to it.

I eased myself into a chair and took another sip. In all my years dealing with human dregs, and with all the Bible classes I had been in, I still could not understand what I knew to be true.

Leaning back, I wiped a hand down my face, pausing to rub my burning eyes, and took another swallow of black death. I shook my head.

Man can be totally depraved.

THREE

I checked my watch. Four A.M. Any time now employees would start streaming in, making the compilation of a list of suspects difficult. I needed to check with the guard at the gate to see what he could tell me about incoming employees during the night. The police would no doubt check the schedules, but that would take a while, and they weren't likely to share it with me. And who said the killer, if he or she were an employee, wouldn't have come in on his day off to do this?

Why was I so interested? Habit, I suppose. Curiosity. Besides, this happened more or less under my nose, and I took that a little personally.

I got up, stretched, and dropped my Styrofoam cup into a trash bin. The thick brown dregs from the bottom of the cup oozed out to mingle with the rest of the garbage. I almost hated throwing away good coffee.

It was still dark as I pushed my way through the squeaking wooden doors of the employee cafeteria. This part of the backstage was isolated from the amusement area. It was filled with portable offices, warehouses, shops and vehicle repair bays. The employees had to walk through this area to get to most of the park. They were required to park their private vehicles in a designated lot across a public street and walk in and out through a guard-controlled gate, showing their park I.D. each and every time.

Naturally, the big wigs were the biggest abusers of the I.D. card rule, and they exempted themselves from this drudgery. Every gate guard was supposed to know them by sight, smile, and wave them through. Naturally the guards got to know, or at least recognize, most of the employees and only checked cards on those who didn't look familiar. Most of the guards became pretty good at remembering faces. Problems arose when employees were terminated. Several had entered the park unauthorized, waved through by guards who weren't aware of it. Fortunately, no mischief had been done. Not, perhaps, until today. Nonetheless, it was always a good practice to make everyone show his or her card.

The times I worked the gate some of the big shots tried to slide past, but I politely asked for their card, and they had to show it. I could tell they were miffed, but, hey! a rule's a rule, I always say. Needless to say, I was not number one on the popularity poll.

But I could live with that. After all, I was just following orders.

As I approached the guard shack I could see Ralph Long leaning back in his chair, his face stuffed in a car magazine. I tiptoed up and rapped suddenly and loudly on the glass. He jerked his head up, a look of fear and guilt on his face that relaxed into a relieved grin when he recognized me.

"Whew!" Ralph exhaled. "I thought you were Brito. He checks up on me a couple times every night."

"Then why were you reading a forbidden periodical?" I asked.

"I wasn't reading!" His voice quieted and he leaned forward. "Between you and me and Harry's microphone, I was catching a little shuteye. I'd rather get yelled at for reading than sleeping, and with my face covered by the magazine that's all they could prove."

"They don't have to prove anything, Ralph. They could lie about it."

His brow furrowed. That was something he hadn't considered.

"Is Brito due by here?" I asked.

"Probably not," Ralph said, checking a scrap of paper on his desk. "He came by at one and again at three. That ought to do it for tonight. Say, do you know what's going on? Why all the cop cars and stuff?"

"Little problem inside. You see anybody come through you don't know?"

"When?"

"Since you came on duty."

"Well, a lot of people came through, both directions. They all had their I.D. badges."

"Nothing unusual?"

"Nope. Why?"

"Do you know a kid named Everett Curran?"

"No. What's he look like?"

Thinking maybe Ralph knew Curran by sight, I gave him the kid's description, where he worked, and the uniform he usually wore.

Ralph shook his head. "Sorry. Doesn't ring a bell."

"Okay, thanks."

"If I see him do you want me to call you?"

Just then the coroner's wagon pulled out from the nearby receiving gate and drove past.

"No need," I said. "There he goes now."

I left Ralph sitting with his mouth open, his unasked questions unanswered, and walked out to the employee parking lot. Wendy had told me the type of car the kid had registered with the personnel department when he got his parking sticker—an '81 Olds Delta 88, brown. Probably a parental hand-me-down. Even kids named Everett didn't buy Oldsmobiles. Volkswagens, Hondas, Toyotas . . . anything small and foreign. That close-up and personal feeling you get from a car that crowds you, sounds like marbles in a tin can and revs real high while going slow.

Saves gas, they would say. Ecology-minded youth. Save the environment. Save the whales. Then they listen to rap music or grunge rock, singers who sound like fingernails on a blackboard. What about noise pollution? Boom boxes? Cars with holes in their mufflers?

I walked past my canary yellow, full-size 1969 American-made van with 150,000 miles on the odometer—a van that gets a delicious eleven miles to the gallon. I smiled and gave it a pat. Honesty, reality, simplicity, utility.

There weren't many cars in the lot yet, and the Delta 88 was easy to spot. It was pretty far out and all by itself, several empty rows past the nearest car. I made my way out to it and peeked in, careful not to touch it. The police obviously hadn't been out here yet and most likely weren't aware of it.

The Olds was locked, as I expected. The seats had cheap auto parts store covers on them, the kind that stretch over the original bench seat. They were a kind of cowboy plaid, multi-colored nylon to go with any color vehicle, the kind of seat covers usually found on old pickups. The interior was clean and empty except for a pile of candy wrappers in the back seat. I wanted to see in the trunk—although I didn't really expect to find anything—but couldn't force it open. Well, I could. I mean, I thought I had better not. Lieutenant Brown would have a fit. I'd just have to wait and find out from him what was inside.

I walked slowly back to the gate trying to figure out why the kid had parked so far away.

Rather than walk past Ralph, I took the long way around: out the driveway, down the street, and back in through the receiving gate. This is where the delivery trucks entered with their merchandise: fresh food for the restaurants (that our cooks turned into garbage), car parts deliveries, even new dinosaurs for the dino ride. Through this gate came the lunch wagon for backstage employees, repairmen for the old dinosaurs, vendors, and salesmen. Whatever was delivered or whomever had business with the park came through here. The big shots and their official guests drove through here also, as well as perimeter security vehicles, the cops, the news media . . . and, of course, the coroner on selected occasions.

The nice thing about the receiving gate is that everyone who came through was logged, except (of course) the park administration and owners. When they brought their cars inside they did the same routine as they did at the employee gate: wave and speed by. I wanted to know who had come through tonight, and I hoped the guard would remember. Generally there wasn't much traffic through here in the wee hours—the hours just before the murder.

The guard saw me coming but didn't get up off his stool. I wasn't that important. As I drew closer, I saw his feet on the counter. He was playing an imaginary guitar to the portable stereo strains of Dire Straits' *Tunnel of Love,* a song about an amusement park romance. I couldn't have planned my arrival better.

"Say, Bert, what's up?" I asked. He gave me the ***wait a minute*** sign as he finished his guitar solo, then reached over and turned the volume down a half-decibel.

Bert was one of the good guys. To him this was just a job, not a stepping stone to law enforcement as many of the officers viewed the position. Bert was happy just to sit in his booth all night long listening to the radio and logging vehicles in and out. It paid his modest bills, put inexpensive clothes on his six-foot-four-inch lanky carcass, kept him in guitar strings, and sometimes—but not too often—paid for a trim of his curly blond hair. He was easy-going and unpretentious, a breath of fresh air in this place, and well-liked by just about everyone.

"What're you doin' out here?" he asked. "I thought you were working inside today." ***Inside*** was park employee lingo for the amusement area the public pays to visit.

"I am," I confirmed. "I just thought I'd putter around a little."

"Anything to do with the cops and coroner?"

"Mmmm."

"What happened, anyway?"

"Tragedy. An employee died in there tonight. Ride operator. Everett Curran. You know him?"

"No, can't say I do. I know more people from Freddy's Fresh Seafood and Meat than I do from here. What happened? He get run over by a log? Knocked off the loading dock by a fat lady into the path of an oncoming six-foot dinosaur egg?"

"Boy, they have stupid ride carts here," I said, shaking my head.

"So . . . ?" Bert urged.

"Nothing quite as glamorous as that. You sure seem cavalier about death."

"Sorry. Death just seems less serious at an amusement park—especially such a poorly-run amusement park like this."

"Bert, you've been here a long time," I observed. "Why do you call this place poorly-run?"

"Like, you don't know?"

"I've got my ideas," I admitted. "I just want to compare notes, see if I'm on the right track."

"It's simple, really. They're too top heavy. There's the owners, a group of people who don't know anything about running an amusement park; a president whose claim to fame is that he used to design miniature golf courses; seven vice-presidents, and on it goes. And only one or two of them are really qualified."

"Is that all?"

"Not by a long shot. There's a lot of good people who work here, but a large percentage of them are doing the wrong job. People with accounting degrees are pushing drinks across counters, artists are wearing bumblebee costumes—shoot, look at you. You've been a cop for all these years, and when there's a sergeant's opening, who gets it? A twenty-year-old fat guy who used to count people as they walk through the front gate."

"I guess I'm not a company man."

"No kidding."

"That's basically what I came up with. And you ought to be in one of the park bands. I understand you're pretty good with a guitar."

"Yeah, I do okay. But it doesn't pay any more than security, and I like the hours better out here." He smiled sarcastically. "Besides, I get to wear this spiffy uniform."

"Looks good on you." I smiled back. "Listen, can you tell me who came in here tonight?"

"Sure." He checked his log book. "Lessee . . . ." He ran his finger down the list. "We had alpha-X-ray-kilo-one-seven-seven, three-romeo-one-seven-six-two-four—"

"What?" I interrupted. "You mean to tell me you only write down the license numbers?"

He looked at me like *of course, what did you expect?,* then broke into a grin. "Just pulling your chain. Three delivery trucks to merchandise, in and out in fifteen minutes; a dead-chicken truck to the restaurant; the laundry service for a pick-up. That's it."

"What about private vehicles. Anybody come in that you didn't log?"

"Sure. Twelve cop cars, the crime scene investigation van, the coroner's wagon, four unmarked cop cars, Harry, John Hayes, Michelle Yokoyama—"

"Vice-president of merchandise?"

"The same."

"What's she doing here at night?"

"Got me. I think she uses her office for entertaining, if you know what I mean."

"It's a sordid world we live in."

Bert nodded in sad agreement.

"Anyone else?" I asked.

"Yeah. Opperman."

"*He* was here?" I was appalled. The president of the place,

Mr. Miniature Golf Course, actually showed up during a crisis. "Was he alone?"

"As far as I could tell."

"That's weird. He never showed up at the mine ride."

"Looked to me like he drove straight to his office. Is that where it happened?"

"His office?"

"No, the mine ride."

"Oh. Yeah, that's where he was found. Okay, man, thanks." I started to walk off.

"Hey! Wait a minute!" Bert yelled after me. "You never told me what happened to the kid."

"Someone corked him one on the head," I said over my retreating shoulder.

"Whoa! And it happened here? While I was sitting in this booth?"

"Looks that way."

His eyes widened and he smiled. "Cool."

I shook my head. Bert led a sheltered life out here at the receiving gate.

As I headed back toward the park, I ran this whole affair through my mind systematically. Who were the suspects . . . so far? It had to be someone who worked here. That narrowed it down to fourteen hundred or so people. They had to have a key to have been able to get into the mine ride. Curran was just a ride operator, not a crew leader or supervisor, so he wouldn't have had one. Shouldn't have, at least.

How about motive? Maybe that would help point to someone. Contrary to popular fiction and television, few murders have a real good motive. At least, they aren't always obvious. Motives are something that are frequently discovered only after the culprit is captured and has confessed. Too often the motive is because the killer is psycho and a voice told him to do it, or he hated his mother and got back at her by killing brown-haired women with skinny legs.

Don't laugh. One serial killer was asked why he picked a

particular house to enter—where he brutality stabbed to death two women he had never met—and he said their door was unlocked. That's it, the only reason. At the first house he went to, the doors were locked, so he didn't feel welcome and went on to the next one where he was "invited" in by the unlocked door.

The murder of Everett Curran, however, was not the work of a serial killer. But it had a motive, I was sure of that. It only appeared senseless because we didn't know what that motive was. And finding the motive would be like finding the killer's name in large, neon letters.

My deep contemplation was interrupted by my portable radio.

"One-thirty-one, come in."

I pulled my radio out of its leather pouch and held it up to my face as I walked in the back door of the security office. I keyed the mike.

"Come in where?" I asked.

"You know what I mean, just answer your radio." It was Brito. He went to the old movie school of radio procedure.

"I didn't hear the question."

"Cut the jokes. I need you here."

"Okay. Where are you?" I moved quietly to the dispatch area, unseen, turned off my radio and put it away.

"In the station."

"Ten four." I said this with my hand over my face to muffle it. I was about four feet behind Brito, who was leaning over Wendy to reach the radio console.

"Okay." He stood up and turned around so abruptly he almost bowled me over.

"Where'd you come from?" Brito asked.

"South Dakota," I said, "but I was little and don't really remem—"

"No, I mean right now."

"You called me in," I said, jogging his memory. "I'da been here sooner but I had a flat."

He grumbled, brushed past me, and trudged into his office. I followed.

"I need you to write a report on finding the dead kid."

"Okay. But why? I already told the cops everything."

"They want it in writing."

"You sure? They usually *don't* want it in writing from the witness. Something the witness writes later might conflict with what they told the cops at the scene and could discredit their testimony in court. You know, poor memory, or they overhear something and later decide they saw it too when they really didn't—"

"Just do it! Harry wants it."

"Ohhhhh, it's for Harry, not the cops. That's different." I paused for a yawn. "Are you sure you want me to do this? I'm pretty emotionally distraught right now."

Brito answered with a glare.

"Okay, no problem. I'm feeling better already. I'll get right on it."

I could feel his stare on my back all the way to the report writing room. They called it a room, at least. It was really more of a wide hallway with a table against one wall holding stacks of report forms.

I grabbed a couple miscellaneous report blanks and sat down. They must have wanted short reports from us because the chairs were unpadded wood, very uncomfortable. The excitement of the morning had kept me going so far, along with my goofing on Brito, which was all in good fun, but by 6 A.M. I was beginning to wear out. Trying to make out a detailed and accurate report without my forehead thumping the tabletop was not going to be easy.

As briefly as I could, without telling Harry more than I thought he should know, I started scratching my account. I approached it as I thought Theo—Lt. Brown—would if he were writing it and what he would include. I left out my journey to the parking lot and my questioning the other guards, as well as the snooping I did inside the ride before I called dispatch. None of this would be important to anyone else. Additionally, I didn't have control over who would read this. You never knew, the killer might have access to a copy. And, after all, everyone was a suspect as far as I was concerned—including Harry. Besides, Harry's only concern was lawsuits and then only because John Hayes was concerned about it. So I gave them the Reader's Digest version.

It didn't take long to complete, seeing as how I left out the most important stuff, and I took it in to Brito. He glanced up sleepily from some papers on his desk.

"Done already?" he asked.

"I came, I saw, I conquered," I said with a shrug. I set the report on his desk on top of his rolled-up gun belt. Brito was a special deputy to the county sheriff and, as such, was permitted to be armed. No one else working at night was so designated, including me. It was an old good ol' boy clause that would probably end when a new county sheriff was elected. You see, he and the guy who founded the park went way back—old cronies that scratched each other's backs.

Only the sergeants had special deputy status, and only the sergeants carried firearms. Probably a good idea considering some of the people they hired to work security. Most of the men and women were okay, but enough of them were unsuitable for carrying a gun to make the restriction necessary.

Not that Brito was suitable. He was made a sergeant because he kissed a lot of rings and didn't make waves. But, all in all, he was relatively harmless and easy to intimidate—and half my age.

He glanced over the report. "Okay, thanks. Looks like it's all there."

"You didn't read it. Are you basing your assessment on the number of pages?"

He looked up at me perturbed. "No. On trust. I know you'll do a good job on something like this."

"Touché, sarge," I said humbly. "I apologize for the sarcasm."

"Yeah, whatever. You going home now?"

"Uh, yeah. Why?"

"I dunno. Just making conversation."

"Oh. Yeah, I thought I would. I'm tired, and I gotta be back here tonight."

"Okay. Good. You look tired." He paused, then added. "Oh, and good job, Gil. See you later."

"Thanks, Jaime."

I walked out feeling a little sorry I had given him such a bad time.

FOUR

I really intended to go home. I was beat. Staying up all night isn't easy even if you have something to do. It's an affront to the body's circadian rhythms. Scientific studies have proven that no amount of sleep during the day can prevent the body from wanting to fall asleep when the sky gets dark and the wee hours tick by.

But I had work to do.

I drove the few blocks to my place and dragged myself inside. After showering—cold, to try and confuse those circadian rhythms—I dressed in civies and went back out to my tank.

Being a childless widower had its benefits: I could eat out whenever I wanted. It's not that I couldn't cook; I just didn't want to bother. I motored into the parking lot of a local cafe to refuel and lay out my battle plan.

Avoiding pancakes, which I dearly love but can't tolerate, I chewed on a grapefruit and drank several gallons of hot black coffee while I doodled some names in my notebook—names of people I needed to talk to. I wasn't in any position to start listing suspects. I didn't have enough paper for that.

The first names—titles, really—that I put down were Everett's bosses. This included his immediate supervisor and department head. I also needed to talk to anyone who worked with him, who knew anything about him: his personal habits, any friends, where he spent his free time, that kind of stuff. I had no idea how big a task this would turn out to be. If this kid was popular, it could be tons. If I was lucky, he'd turn out to be one of those people that no one ever notices. But that was more than I could hope for.

I threw my pen down, rubbed my eyes, and looked around for the waitress with a pitiful look on my face and an empty mug in my hand. She saw me, felt compassion for my plight, and sauntered over with the pot.

"Go home and go to bed, Gil," she suggested.

"Can't, Hollie. Got too much to do." I knew her from my police days. Hollie was one of the good ones, a waitress for whom it was a profession, something she enjoyed doing. And she did it well. She was prompt, courteous, and made you glad you were there. And it was genuine, not just designed to get the big tip. Those kind were obvious. Always the phony grin, overly pleasant yet meaningless chit chat, laughing hard no matter how unfunny your comment. But leave them a small tip and next time, watch out. You'll be wearing part of your dinner—that is, if it's not delivered cold—or wait forever for a refill of your coffee cup. Not Hollie, though. If you stiffed her—and no one ever did—the next time you came in, she'd treat you like you gave her twenty bucks instead of a handful of air.

"What're you working on?" She started to pour the coffee.

"It's a secret."

She stopped pouring.

"Come on, Hollie, give me a break. If I tell you, I'll have to kill you."

Her eyes narrowed and she put her free hand on her hip. "You investigating something for the cops?"

"I'm checking into something, but not for them. It's just something I want to do. You know, get the juices flowing again." She filled the cup.

"Is it big?"

"Murder."

"The kid in the park, right?"

"Yeah. How'd you know?"

"Couple of blue suits were in here a little bit ago. I overheard them talking about it."

"What'd they say?"

"It's a secret. If I tell you, I'll have to kill you."

"That line's copyrighted."

"Maybe, but not by you."

I stuck out my lower lip and pouted.

"Oh, stop with the poochie lips already, Gil. They didn't say anything important. Just that it looked like an insider. Someone who worked at the park."

I took a sip of my coffee and looked thoughtful.

"Is that what your list is?" she prodded. "You're gonna talk to people the kid worked with?"

"Yeah. It's starting to look like a big job."

"Why don't you narrow it down?"

"Nice idea. How?"

"Talk to the people closest to the kid first. May save you some time."

"Like who?"

"You're the detective. Who's closest to any kid his age?"

"His mechanic? His dog? His dermatologist?"

"You're cute, but dumb. I like men like that. No, you big oaf, his girlfriend."

She patted me on the head and walked off to fill other folks' mugs.

Hollie was right, of course. That's the problem with being tired. The brain doesn't always work properly. Her suggestion was obvious.

I left the money for the meal and the tip on the table and waved to Hollie as I walked out. I felt a little better—although I sloshed now—and when I climbed into my van I bowed my head and said a quick prayer asking God for a little wisdom and a lot of energy.

God had taken good care of me in spite of my insistence upon making stupid decisions regarding my job. I always was hardheaded. And despite knowing better, I thought I could run my life better than He could.

Look back over my résumé. You'd see several different law enforcement jobs, but not just because of dissatisfaction with the departments, but because of impatience—thinking I could advance faster in my career if I helped God along by going to a new P.D. every five years. In reality, every time I moved I did so just before a promotional opportunity, so I missed out on what God might have had for me. And it took me several years to figure it out, but by then it was too late.

But I've learned that even though I had placed myself in a negative situation, God would use it to my good. Oh, He wouldn't always let me escape the repercussions for my actions, but whatever punishment life dealt me—most of which I deserved, unlike Joseph or Job—God was always there to comfort and instruct. What I needed to learn was to be content, to make the best of what I had, so I could avoid these bad decisions. Sounds easy, right?

I eased into traffic and headed back to the park. Pulling into the employee lot and parking in the hinterlands, I noticed that Everett's car was gone. Opening time was near, and there were probably six or seven hundred employees here—and few of them carpooled.

I.D.ing my way past the employee gate guard—you never knew when a supervisor was secretly supervising—I ducked back through the backstage area toward the Flapper Zone.

The Flapper Zone was an attempt to capture the excitement of the twenties by cramming as many stereotyped pre-depression era businesses and attractions as possible onto a single city block. The street was an "S" curve unlike any real street of the period, but that concept was utilized throughout the park to create the illusion of distance and separation. There was always another bend in the road and a surprise around it. A few actual cars from the twenties were parked by the curbs here and there, all of them operational. All the employees, whatever their job, wore period costumes: knickers, armbands, knee socks, all kinds of hats. The only exception to this were the security officers who wore the same thing I did. The colors were bright, the neon dazzling, the piped-in music raucous.

The overall effect was pretty good, actually, although overdone and unrealistic. But it set the scene, and no one had a problem figuring out what bit of Americana they were walking through.

To get to the Ride Operations office, I had to pass the Bijou Theater, the Speakeasy Cafe, and the Flapper Flipper, a cheesy throw-up ride right next to the Soup Kitchen, a burger and fries place (but no soup). When I turned the corner into the alley where the office sat disguised as a skid row mission, I was surprised to see Theo Brown headed for it too, from the other direction. Too late, I abruptly turned and started to retreat. He called to me, and I looked around like I didn't know where the voice came from.

When he caught my eye, I looked surprised. "Hey, Theo! Good to see you again so soon! How's the investigation going?"

"What're you doing here?" He was always known for ignoring social pleasantries and getting right to the issue, which made him a good detective and a lousy public relations man.

"I work here."

"Not here, you don't," he said, pointing to the ground. "You work in security, or have you forgotten? Besides, you work nights and wear a uniform. In case you haven't noticed, the sun's out and you're in civvies."

I looked up into the sky, then down at myself, and acted surprised. "You're right, Lieutenant. I should be home asleep. Nice talking to you."

"Not so fast, hot shot. I still want to know what you're doing here. You got an angle on the Curran murder?"

I looked Brown directly in the eye and exhaled heavily. "Not yet, Theo, but I'm trying to find one. How about you?"

"Come on, you're not one of us anymore. As a rule we don't spread our info around to every amateur detective that asks—especially security guards."

He said it with such derision that I was a little taken aback. I hadn't realized he was so bitter. Nor could I figure out why. I decided to explore it.

"What's the problem, Theo? What'd I ever do to you?"

"You left. That's what you did. I was on your side. Defended your idiosyncrasies. Then you up and leave, and my credibility was sucked out the door in your wake."

I was stunned. I had no idea that my abrupt departure from the P.D. had affected anyone else. Suddenly a verse popped into my mind. ***A brother offended is harder to win than a strong city.***

"I'm sorry, Theo. I didn't mean to cause you a problem." I couldn't think of anything else to say.

Theo looked at his shoes for a moment, then broke the awkward silence.

"Ah, you did what you thought was right," he said quietly. He didn't sound won over yet.

"Maybe," I said. "But I wasn't right, and everyone knew it. I didn't think it through. I'll be the first to admit I made a mistake. And now I'm paying the penalty." Sometimes it was better to be open, if not blunt.

Uncomfortable, Theo changed the subject, his tone more subdued. "We haven't discovered anything important yet, Gil, not as far as we can tell. The lab people are going over everything with a fine tooth comb, checking hair fibers and all that. We made casts of every different shoe print we could find within a ten foot diameter of the body."

"Plaster?" I asked.

"No, we're using expanded polyfoam now."

I was impressed. For all the technology out there, it seemed police departments were the last to get a hold of it.

The stuff Theo was talking about has been used by model railroaders for decades to make lightweight rocks and scenery. Two liquids, when poured together into a mold, expand to fill every crevice and crack, then dry in seconds to a hard yet light foam with a skin that is the exact duplicate of the object that was used to make the mold. With the right coloring, the dried polyfoam appears identical, yet weighs only a fraction of the original. It could also be carved into shape. The park used it in large quantities for artificial rocks on the newer indoor rides, replacing the heavy and expensive gunite wherever possible.

"Finally in the twentieth century," I observed to Theo.

He grunted. "You know how it is . . . . Budget constraints."

"I noticed the chief and captains get new cars every year."

"Part of their benefit package."

"Whatever happened to sacrifice? Keep those three big sedans one extra year, the city saves forty-five thousand dollars, one officer's annual salary."

"Shoot, they did that when you left."

"Funny."

"C'mon, you know common sense is irrelevant when it comes to the admin's goodies."

"Like trying to take a bone from a mean dog." I shook my head, and we both fell silent, knowing the conversation was futile. I turned my thoughts back to dead boy, Everett Curran. "Any thoughts on a motive?"

"None that could explain why he was killed. No one I've talked to yet has a clue. I started at the top—"

"Opperman?"

"No, John Hayes. Is there somebody over him?"

"Not that matters. What did Hayes have to say?"

"Not much. Didn't know the kid. Concerned mostly with the park's image. A real caring individual."

"Typical. Anything else?"

"Near as anybody knew, Curran was totally straight-laced. Smart, nondrinker, nonsmoker, didn't sleep around, went to church, worked hard—"

"What a deviant!"

"Mmmm. He certainly swam upstream. I always get suspicious of guys like him."

"*I'm* like him."

"Case closed."

"Come on, Theo. So the kid seems to be straight. What's wrong with that?"

"Unrealistic. In this day and age, no one's a cherry."

"No one's free of sin, Theo, but not everyone has a vice."

"This kid claimed to be a Christian, Gil, did you know that?"

"No," I admitted, "but it doesn't surprise me."

"How so?"

"No vices, right?"

"Right."

"Well, perhaps he did have just one."

"I thought so," Theo said. "What was it?"

"He ate a lot of chocolate bars." I revealed. "Food abuse is common in Christian circles. It's an *acceptable* sin. Overeating is the only thing they can do without guilt. Virtually every church function, no matter what denomination you go to, is accompanied by food of some sort."

"How do you know?"

"I go to church. Take my own table service."

"No, I mean how do you know he indulges in sweets?"

"I peeked in the back seat of his car last night. It was full of candy wrappers."

"Think it means anything?"

"Only that you aren't going to find any skeletons in his closet. Curran was straight, and that's all there is to it."

"Which means . . . ?"

"Which means there has to be a motive for his murder unrelated to sex, drugs, rock and roll, theft, or some criminal act, unless you consider the remote possibility that Curran stumbled into something, like a crime-in-progress. But the trouble someone took dressing his body would tend to rule that out, don't you think? Especially since he was found here and not in some alley. Chances are, Theo, your murderer is not going to be a common, garden-variety criminal."

"We already think it's an employee. Sort of a massive scale locked-room crime, with fourteen hundred people in the room. Besides, don't you think some of the employees here are criminals?"

"Oh, sure. The background checks they do are sketchy at best, nonexistent for the most part. And some of the employees are stealing from the company every time they cash their paycheck. What I mean is, it doesn't look like the kid was snuffed by a common criminal for common criminal reasons, like dope or robbery. I think it may turn out to be something else, by someone you wouldn't normally think capable of murder."

"Industrial espionage?" he asked.

"Could be, something like the—"

A crowd of screaming kids broke in our direction, and there was no escape as they swept around us. I looked up to see what was attracting them and realized we were standing at the entrance to the Midget Dinosaur Kingdom. That wasn't its real name: I added the *Midget* part. You see, they set up this prehistoric atmosphere in a slow, dark ride, then paid millions for some Hollywood company to build moving dinosaurs. When they arrived everyone gasped. Literally. The tyrannosaurus rex was eight feet tall and looked like he belonged in front of a supermarket. And it didn't take long for the dinosaurs to start breaking down. The movie effects people made their stuff to last a few weeks, long enough to shoot the movie, not for an indefinite period and constant daily use. And not just the mechanics went bad. The skin split open; the teeth fell out. They looked like refugees from the old dinosaurs' home.

"It'll be mostly dark in there," one employee said when the dinos were delivered. "Good," someone had answered. "Then no one can see how embarrassed we are." But kids being kids, those under five loved it anyway. To them, the dinosaurs were huge and scary.

I nodded for Theo to follow me and walked over to a popcorn cart. I bought two bags and handed one to him.

"Maybe not industrial espionage exactly," I continued as we sauntered casually down the avenue. "Curran's not the type. And he wasn't robbed, correct?"

"Not that we can tell," Theo answered with his mouth full. "We found his clothes stuffed behind some fake scenery stuff."

"Why change his outfit?"

"To delay his discovery, probably," Theo surmised. "But that didn't work. The killer didn't count on Gil Beckman strolling through there."

I shrugged. "You know, if he hadn't been found till later, you'd have a lot more suspects. Frankly, they should've just stuck him in a dark hole. He'd probably still be there and we'd have another ten thousand suspects."

"The general public?"

"Yeah. Every patron."

"So they goofed," Theo concluded. "Not very well thought out."

"Why do it in there at all?" I asked. "Seems like a lot of trouble to go to."

"Maybe they didn't mean to."

"Didn't mean to kill him? Or didn't mean to kill him in the ride?"

"Take your pick."

"Whichever it was, it certainly wasn't a crime of passion. Whoever killed him—"

"Or *had* him killed," Theo interjected.

"Good point. Whichever, it was an act of desperation and had to be covered up as best they could on the spur of the moment. Somehow, this kid had become a threat to someone." I shook my head and popped a handful of popcorn in my Christian, food-abusing mouth.

Theo pulled a piece of popcorn from between his front teeth while he mulled my theory over. "It wasn't a professional job, that's for sure."

We both fell silent, except for chewing noises which were drowned out by the park guests. Theo eventually threw away his half-eaten bag of popcorn.

"What now?" I asked.

"Tell me what you're after here."

"I don't really know. I was going to talk to some of Curran's co-workers, see if I could come up with a reason someone would kill him."

"Do you know who they are?"

"Maybe by sight at the most. I'll go to the supervisors. With my I.D. card from here I can talk to most of them without suspicion." I paused. "If that's okay with you."

"Tell you what," Theo said. "You go ahead, get what you can here. But if you get a line on something, I want to know pronto. I'll take it from there. Understand?"

"Sure. Thanks."

He handed me his business card after writing something on it.

"That's my pager number. Save you from the hassle of going through the switchboard."

I stuck the card in my wallet. "When did you get pagers?"

"Right after you left."

"Rats," I said, truly disappointed. "I missed out again."

Theo grinned. "Call me, Gil."

I nodded and he left without further comment. I watched him as he strolled through the Flapper Zone, looking every inch the self-assured detective. I then turned and fought my way through the excited crowd. A group of wide-eyed young people hung on each other and jabbered as they bounced up the street, anticipation in their eyes. They obviously hadn't been here before. I envied their innocence as I made my way to the Ride Operations office, hoping I could get something I could sink my teeth into there. Besides popcorn.

FIVE

I found the office door just off the main road through the Zone and pushed it open. A woman I presumed to be a secretary was talking—or rather, consoling—a uniformed female ride operator who seemed unusually distraught, a little blonde in her late teens. The secretary was about thirty-five, nominally attractive and well-dressed. Her hair fell about her shoulders and was a striking reddish-brown that appeared natural. She eyed me suspiciously.

I had obviously barged in on something and wondered if it could be related to the Curran killing. I apologized for the interruption.

"May I help you?" the secretary intoned without acknowledging my apology.

"Yes, maybe you can. I'm Gil Beckman, with park security." I showed her my I.D. card. "I wonder if it would be possible to see Dave Whelan?"

Whelan was the department head in charge of Ride Operations. The operators were the front line, so to speak, of all the park employees. They helped people on and off the rides, pressed the buttons that started each journey, and were basically responsible for everyone's enjoyment and safety while at the park. No small job, and for which, they were paid little more than minimum wage.

Kids with outgoing personalities were preferred for this task, and shy people usually weren't too successful. Whelan himself had started ten years before as an operator and managed to work his way quickly to the top spot, bypassing others just as qualified and with more time on. At least, that's what I'd been told.

"What may I tell him this is in reference to?"

"Well, I'm afraid it's rather sensitive. I'll have to beg your indulgence and tell him that myself." I didn't know who the blonde was, but if she knew Curran, I didn't want to upset her.

"I'll see if I can help you." The secretary was irritated, but I couldn't tell if the source of her irritation was personal or just because she had been interrupted. Regardless, her actually helping me didn't sound too likely.

She got up from the chair next to the blonde and walked back to Whelan's office instead of using the phone. I couldn't figure out why she disliked me. I was used to irritating people on purpose. This was a new experience for me, irritating someone by just showing up.

The blonde glanced up at me with puffy, red eyes. I smiled nonchalantly but she didn't react, just looked away. Her name tag introduced her as Trish.

The secretary returned, ignoring me and going straight to Trish. But Whelan had followed her out and invited me back into his office. I took a seat opposite the desk from him.

Whelan was an ordinary-looking guy, probably would be considered handsome by those keeping tally of that kind of thing. With a full head of thick brown hair combed back in blow-dried waves and precisely trimmed around the edges, he did not look his age. Easily in his late thirties, he looked a decade younger, his erect body in the kind of shape one would expect of someone who spent an hour in the gym every morning—which Whelan did. I had seen him on several occasions on his way to work out, his leather gym bag and water bottle clutched tightly in his hands.

It was just coincidence that I was there to see him. The

gym is next door to my favorite donut shop, a little mom-and-pop place where the cinnamon rolls are about a foot across. Some habits die hard.

Cops and donuts. It's an old saw, but had plenty of truth in it. Where else can cops get a fresh cup of coffee at three in the morning? Besides, there's as many donuts eaten on Sunday morning at the churches in America as there are by graveyard cops.

Not by Whelan, though. White sugar obviously never passed his lips. He was a terminal yuppie. Drove a Volvo, wore silk shirts and power neckties. Master's degree in business administration, and no life experience, no real concept of the horrible things one human being can do to another.

As I jealously admired Whelan, I had a thought, and "accidentally" knocked a pen off his desk. As I bent to retrieve it, I snuck a quick peek under the desk at his shoes. Dress moccasins, square toe, cute little tassels. I chuckled to myself as I realized that I was lapsing back into an old habit: looking at people's shoes. While I was in high school, I got my first job at a chain shoe store in an indoor mall. I got pretty good at recognizing not only our shoes but those of our competitors. The trouble was, I always walked down the sidewalk with my head down, checking out feet. I found a lot of change that way, but missed some great scenery.

Whelan shopped at the malls, bought shoes in the hundred-dollar range, but I doubted he was the killer. Too messy. Oh well.

"This is just terrible," he said when we were settled.

"What's that?" I asked.

"The Curran thing, of course. Isn't that why you're here?"

"Well, yes it is, actually. I'm doing some checking into it."

"Aren't the police handling that?"

"Yes. But the lieutenant in charge of the investigation, Theo Brown, asked me if I could save him some time and get some preliminary information for him. I used to work for the P.D."

"So I've heard."

My fame had preceded me. Actually, despite there being fourteen hundred employees, all the good rumors made the rounds quickly. Apparently I had been one of them. Then I remembered that I had been featured in a small article in the weekly in-house newsletter. "Famous Homicide Detective Comes to Park." It didn't have to be true to make the news here, just semi-interesting.

"Why'd you leave, Mr. Beckman?" he asked.

"Personal reasons," I answered. "Non-disciplinary." Some people sure are nosey. Normally, I would've told him to mind his own business, but if I did that, he probably wouldn't help me.

"So you came here to be a security guard." He almost sounded mocking.

"Yes, and I enjoy it." He was about to push my button but I held my peace. I needed his help.

"Well, what can I do for you, Mr. Beckman?"

"Please, call me Gil."

"All right." He left it at that. Obviously I was to continue calling him Mr. Whelan.

I said, "We need the names of the people who were close to Curran: friends, people he hung with, girlfriend . . . "

"Why?"

Was this guy stupid or just pretending? I tried not to let my irritation show in my voice.

"Lt. Brown would like to get a line, if he could, on why this happened. He's very interested in catching the"

"It was terrible, to be sure." Whelan shook his head slowly. "But what do all those people have to do with an accident?"

I recoiled, leaning back in my chair. Accident? Maybe I was more tired than I thought.

"I'm sorry, Mr. Whelan. Did you just say accident?"

"Of course. Why do you ask?"

He looked at me, completely perplexed. I rubbed the back

of my neck slowly, pondering but not answering. What had Whelan been told? Confronted by my silence he went on.

"Everett Curran was killed in a freak accident. Something fell and struck him on the head . . ." He leaned forward, a questioning look on his face. "Isn't that right?" All of a sudden he wasn't so sure.

"Mr. Whelan, where'd you hear that?"

"That's what we were told at the department head meeting this morning."

"Maybe they're just being cautious," I offered, "until the police find out for sure." Whelan was obviously a company man. I didn't want to imply that he had been lied to by the company.

"You mean there's a possibility it wasn't an accident?"

"Yes, I'm afraid so."

"That means he could have been . . ." He faded out so I said it for him.

"Murdered." Some people just couldn't say the word. Like some people have to say *passed away, expired, gone to their reward,* when the person they are referring to is actually just plain old dead.

Whelan sank back in his chair and sighed. He actually sounded relieved! I was momentarily stunned until I thought about it. If Curran had been killed by an accident, there might have been a safety violation, something that could actually come back to haunt Whelan, maybe even cost him his job, or make him the defendant in a wrongful death suit.

I guessed by Whelan's reaction that he was not the one who killed Curran—if he was the killer, he was also the world's greatest actor—and I decided to take a chance.

Getting up and closing the door, I moved my chair closer to his and leaned over the desk when I sat back down.

"Mr. Whelan, I'll be honest with you. Everett *was* murdered." Whelan's eyes widened. "There's no doubt about it. I was the one who found him." I paused, watching Whelan's eyeballs flutter as the possibilities raced through his head.

"This is terrible!"

He didn't sound very convincing. Oh, I was sure he'd think it was terrible later, even frightening, once the reality set in. But right now, this was good news for him and his job. No industrial accident to put a blot on his record.

"What does this mean?" he asked, trying to grasp all the ramifications at once. But before I could answer, he added, "Does John Hayes know?"

"Yes, he does." I had to tell the truth. Hayes knew but was covering it up, although that made no sense. It would be in the papers tonight. "He came in while the police were still there. Maybe he is just trying to avoid a panic until they know more about how it happened."

However stupid that may sound, it was probably the reason Hayes was keeping the truth to himself. Cover-ups usually do sound stupid later when the truth is known. Remember Watergate? The problem with that logic was that the panic would be greater later on when everyone found out that not only was Curran murdered, but park administration lied about it. Of course, Hayes could always claim ignorance. No one would argue that.

"Boy!" Whelan looked exhausted. He sank deeper into the chair for a moment, and I waited quietly, allowing his own mind to do my work for me. He soon straightened up.

"Exactly how can I help you?" he asked.

"Look, Mr. Whelan, I don't want to frighten you." Actually I did. "But Everett was murdered *here*, inside the mine ride." I had decided to risk confiding in Whelan. My sixth sense told me he wasn't involved. "The killer may be an employee, someone who was known to Everett. I need to know who Everett's friends were, close friends, casual acquaintances, any problems he had, anything you can tell me that can lead us to his killer."

"To be honest, I don't know that much about him. He was a quiet kid."

"So I've heard."

"You know, the ones who might be able to tell you about him are his supervisor or team leader. They'd know more about the kid." He opened a desk drawer and pulled out a manila folder. Inside was what appeared to be a work schedule. Whelan ran his finger down it, stopping a couple times, then scratched something onto a memo pad, tore it off, and handed it to me. I looked down at a name.

"Denise is his team leader. She'd know more than anybody. She's here today. You'll have to ask around for her, though. She's somewhere in the Future." Then added, "Future Zone, that is, where they have the space rides and carnival games."

"Where should I start?" I asked.

"There's a break room behind Star Tracks. That's where they all hang out."

"Thanks, I'm familiar with it." I'd bought candy bars there in the middle of the night many times. I got up to leave and extended my hand. When Whelan took it, I held on and leaned toward him.

"Listen, Mr. Whelan, this is important. Do me a favor and keep this murder thing under your hat for awhile. As far as we're concerned, the murderer could be anybody. Might even be your secretary." I wasn't exaggerating. She tried to kill me with a look when I came in.

"Oh, um, okay."

"I'm serious, Mr. Whelan. Don't even let on that there's anything happening. It was an unfortunate accident. If the killer thinks you know it was murder so soon after the event, he might also assume you know who did it." Of course that was ridiculous, but I was hoping Whelan wouldn't think so.

"Mum's the word," Whelan whispered. "You can count on me."

"I knew I could."

I left him in his office and walked back out to the secretary's desk, hoping to get there before he told her everything. I noticed the name plate on her desk. Lois Schilling. The blonde was gone, and Lois was seated behind her desk, eyeing me.

I put on my biggest grin. "Miss Schilling, I do appreciate your help today. And I apologize for my untimely arrival. If I had known you were involved, I would have waited before barging in."

She was slightly taken aback. "Oh . . . uh, no problem. It wasn't your fault."

I know that! I thought. So why were you so upset with me? As if reading my mind, she continued.

"I thought you were here for—-well, forget it. I'm sorry."

Interesting. What did she think I was here for? And why did she no longer think it? Had she somehow been listening to us?

"You thought I was here for what?"

"Oh, I don't know. Things are a little strange around here today."

"The Everett Curran thing?" I suggested. She nodded. "That was terrible, wasn't it?"

"Mind boggling," she admitted. "He was such a nice kid. Never any trouble. This kind of accident will not look good on Dave's—Mr. Whelan's record."

So that was it. She thought I was investigating the accident that would be detrimental to her boss, and, therefore, to her. Was she in love with him? Or was it just loyalty? Hard to tell sometimes, the way people act.

"What made you realize I wasn't here to put the screws on your boss?"

She laughed nervously, caught in her misconception. "Accident review isn't handled by security. Took me a minute to remember that, what with Trish here all upset and distracting me. She's completely crazy over the accident. She was the only close friend Everett had."

"That was Curran's girlfriend?" I had let her slip through my fingers. I was disgusted at myself. I should known. Why else would she be in here all upset.

"Yes, yes it was. Why?"

"Oh, no reason. Too bad. Well, thanks, you've been a great help." Without any more comment, I left the office. Leaving a puzzled Lois Schilling staring after me, I took the most direct route toward the employee parking lot. Trish would be going home. I couldn't imagine the girl staying here to work at the place where the love of her life was killed. Not ever, but especially not today.

Wading through the crowd was difficult, as always. Trish didn't know I was trying to catch up to her, though, so she wouldn't be trying to avoid me.

I didn't know how long of a head start she had, but it couldn't have been much. And I didn't notice a purse when she was in the rides office, so maybe she had to stop off at her locker for it. Not knowing where that was, I headed straight for the employee lot.

As I neared the exit, I saw her. I had guessed right when I figured she'd go home. Who wouldn't? She probably had just reported for work and was told to see Lois, or maybe she hadn't heard from Everett and went in to check on him.

Suddenly I understood Lois' attitude. She had just told a young girl that her boyfriend was dead, and I walk in, not only intruding on a difficult scene, but to nail her boss—or so she thought. Maybe she wasn't a bad egg after all, but the kind of secretary most bosses crave: loyal and perceptive.

I caught a glimpse of Trish as she slipped out through the employee gate. She glanced back but was oblivious to me. The morning sun reflected off the tears streaming down her face. I hurried to catch up, but a pack of boy scouts suddenly swarmed out of a gift shop and blew past me like a cattle stampede.

By the time I had waded through them, emerging with two suckers stuck to my pants, she had disappeared. I sighed and decided to let it go for now. She was in shock and probably not all that talkative at the moment anyway. I could find her later.

Weary from lack of sleep, I turned and began moving doggedly back to the Future . . . Zone. Seeing the park perimeter transport out of the corner of my eye, I turned left at the Bijou, the park's version of a live-action theater, and tried to beat the transport to the station.

The transport was really nothing more than a narrow gauge train line with several different styles of engines, including one that looked like a rocket from some 1960s B movie, all pulling nondescript passenger platforms. It wheezed into the station—-in reality a custodial storage room—-and I hopped on board.

Fourteen elderly ladies got on after me, so there was a slight delay before we blasted off once again. I used the extra minute to lean back and close my eyes momentarily. At least, it was supposed to be momentarily. Before I knew it, I was being nudged in the ribs.

"W-wha—? Huh?"

"Wake up, young man. We're here."

I forced open my protesting eyes, struggling to recall where I was and wondering who would call me "young man." It all came to me in a second, and I watched the women hobble off the train, chattering like schoolgirls. I had to grin as they headed straight to Star Tracks, the fastest ride in the park.

I pushed myself up and stepped onto the platform, wishing Curran was alive, and I was in bed. Working tonight was going to be tough.

Finding the break room behind Star Tracks was easy. I could find it in my sleep. In fact, I had on several occasions. When I walked in, I was greeted by some icy stares. What was this *guest*, as the park patrons were called, doing in an employee break room? How dare he?

Before anyone could speak, I answered their questions.

"Park security," I said, holding up my I.D. I quickly scanned the name tags but did not see the one I was looking for. "Can anyone tell me where I can find Denise?"

"Denise who?" A young Latino girl with big, dark eyes

and a toothy smile was behind the question. She was short and petite, and if I were her father, I wouldn't let her out of my sight. There were two other girls with her, one Caucasian and one Oriental who was most likely Chinese-American. And a white male sitting off by himself. I'll say one thing for the park, it's a real melting pot.

I eased myself into the room. "I don't know her last name. She's a team leader."

"Denise Moffat," said the white male. He looked every inch the surf dude with his bleach blond hair, short on the side, long in front; tan; attitude. He also looked familiar.

"Okay, Denise Moffat. Where is she?"

"What'd she do?"

"You her lawyer?"

"Just asking."

"Just don't."

"Why are you copping an attitude, dude?"

"Why are you sticking your nose where it doesn't belong . . . dude?" All I had done was ask where a girl was. What's the matter with kids these days? Where do they get the notion they can talk this way to grown-ups?

"Why don't you blow it out your—"

"Watch your tongue, pal," I interrupted. "There's ladies present."

"Up yours."

I walked up to him and read his name tag. "Joey," I said quietly and wrote it down in my pocket notebook. "Do you need this job, Joey?"

"I couldn't care less."

"Good. Because in five minutes, you won't have it. When I come back from calling Mr. Whelan, you can pack your gear and wave good-bye. This park doesn't need jerks like you."

I turned and walked outside. Before I had gone five steps, he ran out the door and caught up with me.

"Hey, wait a minute!"

I kept walking.

"C'mon, stop a second." He was begging now. "Please?"

I stopped. "Ah, the magic word."

"Are you really gonna call Whelan?"

"Yeah. If you don't believe me you can dial the number."

"Listen, please don't do that."

"Why not?'

"I . . . uh . . . my dad would kill me."

"What you mean, Joey, is that holding a job is a condition of your probation, and if you mess up here and get canned you'll do some time at the youth authority camp in Mojave! Then, when you get out of there, your dad will kill you! Isn't that right?"

Joey the surf-dude Duncan stood motionless, stunned and defeated, his mouth open.

"How'd you know that?"

"Look closely, bwana. I was the one who put your hips in jail in the first place. I was the one who caught you coming out of someone else's house with their VCR in your hands and their blood on your shirt."

"They weren't hurt bad," he interrupted.

Ignoring him, I continued. "I was the one who chased you for five blocks, over two fences, and through a rose garden. I was the one who wiped your spit off my face then *didn't* beat your skull in for the insult."

"S-sorry. I didn't recognize you without your uniform on," he mumbled.

"What was that?" I asked abruptly. "Your lips were moving but I didn't hear anything."

"I said I'm sorry. I didn't know it was you."

"I don't look the same. You aged me." I caught his eye and held it. "Besides, what's that got to do with the way you talk to people? It's time you learned a thing or two."

I turned abruptly and headed for the nearest park phone.

"No, wait! C'mon, give me a chance!"

"You had a chance and you blew it."

"Okay, I blew it. Give me one more chance, *please*!"

I stopped. "Okay, let's see how serious you are. We're going to walk back into that room together and you're going to apologize to me and those girls."

"You're kidding!"

"I am? I could've sworn I was serious."

"I can't do that!"

"Why not?"

He pawed the ground but didn't answer.

"Because it's hard?" I offered. "It'll ruin your tough-guy image? You'll be embarrassed? Let me tell you something, Joey-boy. You think you're a tough guy, really cool, but you're nothing! A real man admits when he's wrong and corrects his mistakes. You're nothing but a pip-squeak. An out-of-work pip-squeak." Once again, I turned.

"Okay, I'll do it," he said.

"That's not all you're going to do," I said as I whirled back to face him.

"What else?"

"You're going to change your whole attitude, start working hard, start being polite, stop swearing, and stop acting like such a tough guy."

There was silence for a moment before he quietly replied, "I'll try."

I shook my head. "Not good enough."

"What do you mean?"

"Trying isn't enough. It leaves you the option of failing, and if you *can* fail, you will. Well, you're not going to fail. You're going to be successful. If you want to avoid hell-camp and avoid being killed by your father, you'll have to decide right now to *do* it, not *try* to do it. And I'm giving you fifteen seconds to decide. Live or die?" I looked at my watch.

Joey was frantic. I meant every word I said, and if he chose wrong, I'd follow through. I could convince Whelan to can him, and his probation officer was a friend of mine, a former cop I once worked with. Don't think I was being overly-harsh with the kid. He desperately needed someone to give him a choice like this. He was constantly being left to his own, and when he failed, his father beat him then let him go out and do it again. I couldn't straighten out his dad, so I did the next best thing. Frankly, I hoped he'd make the right choice, but part of me, to be honest, didn't care. If he was in the youth authority camp in Mojave, maybe he'd learn.

I could hear everything going through his mind. He doubted his own ability to be successful. I did, too. It's our nature to do what's wrong even when we want to do what's right—especially if we have a pattern of doing what's wrong. But in Christ we have help. I had a plan, but I couldn't force it on him. He didn't know it yet, but if he decided to make the right choice, I was going to be there to help.

Frankly, I was surprised I had gotten this far with him. Usually, threatening kids like Joey didn't work. They'd just snort and let you do what you wanted, and if they got fired, they couldn't care less. No, there was something making Joey nervous, something he had neglected to mention. I wondered what it was, then remembered the cute Latino girl. Was it my imagination or were she and Joey making that special kind of eye contact when I first walked in?

I recalled the last kid I had given a choice like this. He had smacked his sister around—for the second time—and his mother, a single parent, was at her wits' end. So I told the seventeen-year-old, either join the army or go to jail. And I meant it. His mom backed me up and said she'd sign the complaint. I don't think the department would have approved, but I didn't tell them. Sometimes proper procedure is ineffective, and what's called for is creativity. Well, he opted to join the army. I saw him six months later, home on leave. He was a man. It had actually worked, and all three of them were grateful.

Joey's seconds were ticking away. "Six . . . five . . . four . . . three . . ."

"Okay, I'll do it!" He was almost crying.

"Okay, Joey. Let's go back to the break room."

He followed me back and the girls were still there. They

were surprised to see us and had obviously been discussing Joey because when we walked in, they immediately stopped talking. All eyes were on us. They could sense something was about to happen. Maybe it was Joey's hunched shoulders and dragging chin.

He stepped forward.

"I . . . I'd like to . . . apologize to you girls for the way I talk in front of you." He looked up in my direction. "And to you for the things I said."

"Accepted," I replied.

The girls' mouths dropped open and one of them finally spoke. It was the Latino cutie. "Okay, Joey, thank you." I'd swear her eye gleamed at my young surf dude.

I let Joey stew in his own juice for a minute, then changed the subject. "Okay. That's over with. Now, where can I find Denise?"

"She'll probably be in the Galaxy Cruiser control room," said the Chinese-American gal.

"Thanks." I left, nodding for Joey to follow me. As we walked out I could hear the conversation start up behind us.

"There, that wasn't so bad," I told him when we were alone.

"Not for you."

I laughed. "That's what I meant. Listen Joey, if you straighten up, you won't have to do that very much."

"Yeah." He was giving me a hard stare.

"What's your problem now?" I asked.

"You gonna hold this over my head forever?"

"If I have to."

"That's not fair!"

"Why not?"

"It's too hard to do things your way all the time."

"I know. Tell me, you doing anything next Sunday?"

"No. Why?"

"Think your dad would mind if you hang around with me awhile that afternoon?"

"He couldn't care less. I might, though."

"Good," I said, ignoring his last comment. "I'll pick you up at one. Don't eat lunch first. I'll treat. You still live in the same place?"

"No, we won the lottery and we live on the hill now. What do you think?"

"Okay. See you then. Now, don't you have to get back to work?"

"Yeah."

"Go on, then. And smile."

I grinned to show him how it's done and watched as he walked hesitantly away, not really knowing what to think of me. That was okay, though. I didn't want him to have me figured out. And the more he tried, the less likely he was to forget about me altogether. Right now he was a lump of hard clay. First, I was going to have to soften him up a bit, then let a friend of mine work on him, my friend Paul—as in St. Paul. He had the same kind of problem as Joey—doing what he didn't want to do and not doing what he should.

And to be completely candid, sometimes, so did I.

SIX

Free to return to the business at hand, I hustled to the Galaxy Cruiser. What a joke this was! A million-dollar throw-up ride that looked like an octopus holding a football in each outstretched tentacle while spinning around and moving each arm up and down and rotating the footballs.

Oh, the riders saw stars all right.

I found the door to the control booth and knocked. A tall girl in her early twenties—a woman really, but with a girl-like face—cracked the door open. Her name tag remained hidden.

"Denise?"

"Yes."

I showed her my I.D. "May I talk to you for a few minutes? It's about Everett Curran."

"Oh." She opened the door and backed up, then closed it behind me when I was all the way inside. The day was beginning to warm up, and she had turned on a small air conditioner. I sat as close to it as possible so the cold air could keep me awake.

"It's really dreadful what happened to Everett," she offered.

"Yeah, it's too bad. I'm trying to help the police with this. Mr. Whelan said you'd be the one to talk to."

"I'll do what I can. But why are the police investigating this? Everyone says it was an industrial accident."

I could tell Denise was smart just by the way she conversed and the way she picked up on that seeming incongruity. It wouldn't do to hide the truth from her. Besides, the evening paper would have the real story. They'd get it off the police dispatch log and Theo's press release. Then they'd come and talk to the park's public information officer. I was confident they'd do everything they could to deny that Curran was killed in the park, like implying he was killed somewhere else then brought here.

No matter what they said, the fact that Curran was murdered would soon be public. I figured I might as well level with Denise. I laughed silently at myself. So far, I hadn't been able to keep the secret I was asking others to keep.

"Denise, do you have a few minutes where we won't be interrupted?"

"Ray's operating the ride. I've got as long as you want. This is serious, isn't it."

"Yes, Denise, it is."

"It wasn't an accident, was it."

"What makes you think that?"

"Come on. You work here. Management said it was an accident. That's enough to make me doubt it. And they didn't give any details. I'm always suspicious when people don't tell me everything."

That settled it. I was going to have to tell Denise everything.

"Denise, Everett was murdered." She sat down hard on a nearby chair. "Clubbed in the head," I continued.

"Here? At the park?"

"Most likely."

"It's so hard to believe."

"I need your help, Denise. Can you tell me who Everett's friends were? Acquaintances? Anyone you think would want him dead?"

"Nobody! He was a nice, quiet kid."

I was beginning to think Everett was either a saint or a sociopath. Serial killers are usually described as "quiet" people, always keeping to themselves. Right. Because they're usually too busy killing people and cutting newspaper clippings to have a social life.

Denise continued. "He didn't have any enemies. He didn't have many friends, either. At least, not any close ones."

"What about Trish?"

"Oh, she liked him a lot. They were good friends, but I don't think you'd classify them as boyfriend and girlfriend. He was too busy with his artwork to take time out for lust." She laughed half-heartedly.

"He was an artist?"

"Trish mentioned it a few times. He was a writer, too, but I have no idea how into it he was, or how good. He never had much time for Trish, though, I know that. She confided in me a little when she was depressed. Trish really liked him. I think she looked beyond his peculiarities and was content to wait until he opened up to her."

"Was he into drugs?"

Denise laughed. "Look, I can't say for sure, you know, but I'd be mighty surprised. I never noticed anything like that. He didn't drink or smoke. I don't think he and Trish had ever even kissed. They were buddies. I think he knew she was a girl, but it never dawned on him that he could have sat in the back seat and made out with her."

"I guess that rules out drug dealing and organized crime."

She nodded, then looked up at me with her brow furrowed. "Who would want to kill a kid like Everett? Who could do such a thing?"

"I don't know yet, Denise. But I aim to find out. Thanks for your help. If you think of anything else, could you give me a call? Here's my number."

She took my card.

"Oh yeah," I said, remembering. "What is Trish's last name?"

"Smith. Spelled the normal way."

"Thanks. And please do me a favor. Keep this conversation to yourself. The person responsible for this just might work here." There was no doubt in my mind, but I didn't want to sound too alarming.

She looked shocked, then nodded. "Makes sense. Could be anybody, couldn't it?"

"Anybody."

"Even you."

"Well, I've ruled me out," I said. "But not you."

We grinned at each other and I left.

I trudged through the park trying to figure out my next move. The list of people to talk to who might shed some light on Everett Curran had just been seriously depleted. Apparently no one but Trish really knew anything about him. Unfortunately, the list of suspects hadn't shrunk. It still included everyone but me. At least, *my* list didn't include me.

Rounding a bend rife with foliage, the pavement changed from painted asphalt to brick, and the buildings from outer space chic to quaint European village. They were nondescript brick and stucco edifices, some with phony thatched roofs, others with tile, and still others covered with irregular wood shingles. No country of origin could be discerned, just somewhere in Europe a hundred or five hundred years ago. This area was home to artisans and craftsmen, little curio shops, and Mediterranean delicacies and desserts. Peasant blouses and large-brimmed hats and suspenders abounded. It was called the Old Country by the park, but renamed by the employees . . . you guessed it—Odd Country.

As I strolled alongside the tulip beds, I listened to the piped in balalaikas and accordions, and smelled sausages and hot Danish buns and baklava while attempting to analyze this situation logically, which wasn't easy with my senses under assault. My stomach reminded me of its presence, but I pressed on. Down boy.

Everett Curran was clubbed on the head, perhaps somewhere inside the mine ride. There was no apparent motive, and it was probably premeditated, a supposition I came up with based on the location the crime occurred and the efforts of the perpetrator to delay discovery of the body. That, and the fact that Everett had no business being there. *Why was he there?*

Everett kept to himself, was apparently not intentionally involved in criminal activity, and had no enemies as far as anyone knew.

Yet someone wanted him dead. He knew something, saw something, heard something, or was in someone's way.

I shook my head. Still too many possibilities. Who stood to benefit from Everett Curran's death? And how? I remembered he still lived at home. His parents. Maybe they could help. And I needed to find Trish. None of them would be easy to get anything out of. They would all be upset, and talking to them would be a very touchy situation.

But now that I had thought it through, something told me time was of the essence. If Everett and Trish were so close, and she was his only friend, maybe she knew what he did to get himself killed. If that was true, and the killer knew it, that might make her the next target.

I had to find her soon, whether she was emotionally up to it or not.

Putting it in high gear, I hurried to the security office and made my way to the dispatch area.

"Sally!" I said when I caught the day shift dispatcher's eye. "You look great today! Is that a new dress? It looks wonderful on you!"

It did, actually, although I laid it on a little too thick to sound sincere. She was a strong woman, not in the physical sense actually, but emotionally and spiritually. Her five-foot-six-inch frame was sturdy, without any excess, at least, anywhere I could notice and still remain a gentleman. Unusual pale hazel eyes that appeared green or brown depending on reflected light, peered out through delicate metal-framed glasses and were shaded by medium-sized, completely natural eyebrows that stood out from her perfect, wrinkle-free skin. Well, maybe there were some laugh lines at the outer corners of her eyes. With a straight nose, full lips, and high cheek-bones, it's a wonder I had hardly ever noticed her. She wasn't what you would call beautiful, but you'd be hard pressed to find anything to complain about.

We had something in common, actually, and had once talked about it. Neither of us had children, and we both had lost our spouses. Mine to illness, hers to divorce. She was a victim, a good woman dumped by a selfish man, a deacon in their church who ran off with the organist. But Sally never expressed any bitterness, only concern for the man who had thrown her away like so much garbage.

Remaining single had been a choice, she told me, not that there hadn't been suitors. She felt she would be inclined to take him back at any time he chose to return. He never did. She found out a year back that he had remarried (not to the former organist), and now she was quite used to the single life and enjoying it in the Lord. She was content.

Sally eyed me with friendly distrust, knowing my compliment to be a ploy to soften her up.

"What do you want, Gil? And for that matter, what are you doing here? Don't you work tonight? You ought to be asleep."

"You're telling me." I fell into hushed tones. "I'm working on something. But it's a secret. If I tell you, I'll—"

"Have to kill me," she sighed. "Right. So, what can I do for you?"

"I need the home address for a ride operator named Trish Smith."

She wrote it down. "Age?"

"Eighteen or so. Maybe nineteen."

"A little young for you, don't you think?"

"This is strictly park business."

"Then it can't be a secret. I know all park business. It's my job."

"Okay, it's police business."

"Then why are you involved?"

"Aw, come on, Sally. If you help me now without any questions, I promise to take you out to dinner and tell you all about it later. It really is important."

She considered me for a moment, her lips pursed.

"A dress-up place?"

I sighed. "Okay, a dress-up place."

I know what you're thinking. Not a good way for a Christian to be conducting his social life. Truth is, Sally went to my church, and I had been wanting to ask her out for some time. I just always thought she'd turn me down.

She smiled. "You're on." She turned to her computer and quickly tapped in a few commands. Accessing personnel records, she located the Smiths and scrolled down the names.

"No Trish," Sally declared. "How about Patricia?"

"Try it."

She checked again. "No luck."

"It must be a nickname. Can we just check all the Smiths? One at a time?"

"I don't have time for that, and you're not authorized to use the computer."

"What do you suggest? Can you use another criteria? Like all female Smiths who work for rides?"

"I'll give it a shot."

Her fingers flew over the keys and in a few minutes we had narrowed it down to sixteen. There were six that matched the age criteria. Sally printed out their files for me.

"Harry's due back from lunch," she warned. "Take these and go."

"One more thing. Give me a printout on Everett Curran."

"Is that what you're doing?"

"Over dinner, remember?"

She smiled, typed on the keyboard, then knit her perfect eyebrows together.

"He's not in here."

"What?"

"His file's been closed."

"Already? Boy, they move fast in personnel."

"What did you need?"

"His address."

"The cops have it. Ask them, since you're working with them."

"Take too long to cut through their red tape."

Sally shrugged. "I don't know what to tell you—wait a minute. Stay here and watch the radio for me." She hurried out of the room. The radio crackled several times as I stared at it intently.

She returned with a photocopy in hand. It was Curran's personnel file.

"Wendy attached it to your report this morning before she left. I recalled seeing her do it."

"Won't Harry miss it?"

"Probably not, even if I had taken the original. But this is just a copy."

"Sally, you're the greatest. Thanks." I put my arm around her shoulders and gave her a squeeze, then started out the door.

"I want a corsage!" she called out after me. I smiled and waved through the window. Hmm, I thought, an old-fashioned girl. What a refreshing surprise.

SEVEN

Sliding into my van in the employee lot, I began pouring over the Smith printouts. Mary, Amber, Beatrice, Lynn, Ashley, Molly. Baby boomers. None of the printouts included physical descriptions, and all the girls were about the same age as the blonde I had seen in Whelan's office. There was little I could use.

I could have made a few more inquiries of Whelan, or perhaps Lois Schilling, but I didn't want to raise too much interest in Trish if I could help it. I didn't know whether the murderer knew about her or not, and I'd feel really bad if I had been the one to tip him—or her—off about the girl.

I checked Curran's address and compared it to all the Smiths. Something told me they lived relatively close to each other. Just a hunch, really, but I couldn't see Everett driving great distances to be with someone he thought of as a "buddy."

I arranged the printouts in order, based on how close they lived to Curran, closest on top. There was nothing else to do but attack it systematically.

As I exited the employee lot, I saw Hayes's Mercedes pull into the receiving gate. Harry was with him. They had probably been discussing their strategy over lunch on how to minimize the negative impact on the park once this hit the news.

I drove past the Curran house on the way to the first Smith

house. It was on a quiet, residential street, very "American." Everett's Delta 88, still covered with fingerprint powder, was in the driveway in front of a newer Delta 88—the same color.

I smiled at myself for pegging Everett's car as a hand-me-down. His parents were obviously creatures of habit. Or maybe Mr. Curran worked for an Olds dealer.

Although anxious to talk to them, I thought Trish was more important. I noticed as I passed that there were fresh tire tracks in the wet gutter in front of their house. As the street was empty of cars, and there was plenty of parking, it didn't seem likely that the car that had been there was for a neighbor. Someone must've just left the Currans' house: a friend, relative, cop. All an assumption, of course, but a safe one.

The first Smith house was only three blocks away. Being in the same tract as Everett's, it was a similar structure: clapboard siding; wood-framed, vertically-sliding windows; real brick chimney; small, single-car garage; and shake roof. There was an old Volkswagen parked out front with a Greenpeace sticker on the bumper, next to a *Save the Whales* sticker. On the other side of the bumper was a pro-choice sticker. Save the whales, kill the babies. Just great. I shook my head, still unable to understand the logic behind their thinking. Oh, I'm all for saving the whales. But a human life is intrinsically more valuable, isn't it?

As I drove slowly past, the front door opened and a tall, slightly overweight brunette in a Solomon's Mine uniform bounced down the steps and toward the car. Strike one, and I was thankful for it. I moved on to number two.

Smith house the second was a bit more upscale. It had a tile roof, skylights, a landscaped yard and a three-car garage. There were several cars in the driveway, one, a red four-by-four pickup. You know, the kind that require a stepladder to get into and are never, ever driven off-road.

I parked in front, checked my printout, and walked through the dead leaves that covered the flagstone walk to the door, a heavy-looking double affair with leaded glass inserts that you couldn't see through. Inside, a stereo was playing loudly, so I knocked hard. When there was no response, I waited until the song was over and tried again. This time the door opened.

"Yeah?" It was a teenage male who looked like he had just stepped off a bus stop billboard ad for one of those trendy, youth-oriented clothes companies.

"Hi," I said, smiling. "Is Lynn Smith here? I work at the park in security."

"What do you want?"

"I just need to talk to her for a minute."

"You don't know Lynn, do you?"

"No, no I don't. I—"

"What's this all about?"

"I just need to ask her a few questions. Park business."

"Lynn's not a 'her.'"

"Huh?"

"I'm Lynn. Do you still need to talk to me?"

I laughed. "No, I don't. You know, personnel lists you as a female."

"Happens all the time." He started to shut the door.

"Hey, wait a sec!" I said. "Maybe you can help me."

"What?"

"I'm really looking for Trish Smith, but that's not her real name and park records don't show nicknames. Do you know her?"

"I've heard of her."

"Do you know her real name, where she lives?"

"No. All I know is she's always hanging around with Everett, uh . . . Kern, Koran—"

"Curran."

"Yeah, that's it."

"Okay, well, thanks anyway, I appreciate the help." He obviously hadn't heard about the murder. "Say, maybe you could help me one more time. I'd really appreciate it . . . . So would Mr. Whelan."

He looked interested. Evidently Lynn Smith could use some brownie points with the boss.

"If I help you, you'll tell Whelan?"

"Sure."

"Okay, what do you need?"

"There's four other Smiths that could be Trish. Maybe you can eliminate the ones you know."

"Let me see your list."

I showed him the printouts. He mulled them over slowly and separated them into two stacks.

"Definitely not," he said, handing me two of them. "Gotta be one of these." He gave me the remaining printouts. Beatrice and Ashley.

"Thanks, that'll really help. I'll tell Whelan tomorrow what a help you've been."

"Thanks. I could use something good in my file."

"Having a tough time?"

"Yeah. A run of bad luck."

"Too bad. Hope this good word can turn it around for you."

"Me too. Say, what's this all about, anyway?"

I figured I might as well tell him. "Everett Curran is . . . uh, I'm afraid he's dead."

"Wow! What happened? Car crash?"

"No. Problem at the park."

"I knew it!"

"What?"

"It had to happen sooner or later."

"What do you mean?"

"It was a ride accident, right? Some of that stuff is really old. We've complained about it being too dangerous. Like Solomon's Mine. What a deathtrap! You ever been in there? There's loose stuff all over the place, old pieces of iron hanging down. They ought to tear it down and start over."

"Isn't it the oldest dark ride in the park?"

"I don't know. I'm not old enough to remember." The way he said it sounded as if he was implying that I was.

"Well, I appreciate your help," I said, turning to leave.

"You'll tell Whelan?"

"Absolutely. I'll write him a letter so he has something to slip in your personnel jacket."

"Thanks." He shut the door and the music came back on.

I sat in my van in front of Lynn's house for a few minutes, looking over the remaining Smiths. They were both fairly close and nothing stood out on the computer printouts that would give me a clue which was the right one.

Leaning back in the driver's seat I closed my eyes and wished I was in bed. I needed sleep. I wasn't as young as I used to be—who is?—and I had a tougher time now staying up more than twenty-four hours than I used to. My record was sixty-two, but I was a basket case for the last ten hours of that and sick for a week afterward. I caught the bad guy, but the quality of my work wasn't up to my normal standards.

As it was now, I hadn't even passed the twenty hour mark. Pretty soon I expected to get my second wind. That would carry me five or six hours, but then it would be time to go back to work.

My mind began to wander. This was nuts. Why wasn't I home in bed? I didn't have to do this. I was no longer a cop. No one was paying me to play detective.

The reality of my bad decision—leaving the P.D.—came rushing in like a dog escaping the rain, stopping only to shake and contaminate everything. A few years ago, I would have been getting paid for this.

What a moron. I wiped both hands down my face and forced my chin into my chest to stretch the back of my neck. Go home, I told myself. Let Theo handle it. He's capable.

But I didn't. I couldn't. Everett Curran had gotten under my skin. It was all I could do to open my eyes again and start the engine. I shifted into drive, rolled down the window, took a deep breath, and pulled away from the curb.

There was no one home at the next house, no cars in the

driveway. Disappointed because I couldn't eliminate Ashley, I moved doggedly to the next Smith.

This house was in an upper-middle class neighborhood. Although they were tract homes, each was customized and didn't have that cookie-cutter look. This particular Smith house was a two-story job with a three-car garage behind the house and a terraced yard. A BMW was in the long driveway, and as I walked up the curving, brick front walk I could hear noise in the house—nondescript household noise indicating someone was inside.

I rang the doorbell and listened to a few bars of *America the Beautiful.* The noises stopped, but the door was not answered. I listened. Nothing. Out of the corner of my eye I thought I saw a curtain move slightly, but when I turned to look, it was still. Probably just my imagination, fueled by fatigue.

I turned to leave, then glanced at the curtain again. This time there was no mistake. It moved. Someone had been peeking out at me. Ringing the doorbell again seemed pointless. They knew I was here. I had the feeling this was the right house, so I decided to take a chance.

"Trish? Trish Smith?" I shouted. "I need to speak to you. It's about Everett!" There was no response. "I'm with park security. You saw me today in Mr. Whelan's office." Still no answer, but I heard the distinctive sound of the BMW starting, then backing out fast. I ran over to the driveway as the Beamer hit the street, shouting for it to stop. It did, but only to allow the driver to shift into first. She cast a panicked glance in my direction as she peeled out, and I was suddenly excited. It was the blonde I had seen in the ride office. Trish.

I ran to my van and jumped in, even though I knew I couldn't catch her. Still, I followed, pushing my six-cylinder, bullet-proof American-made wonder car to its limit. Which wasn't much.

She had turned left at the first corner, and I did so, too, hoping to at least get a glimpse of her. I was surprised to see her only a couple blocks ahead of me, in clear view, traveling at a normal speed. I should have smelled something, but fatigue and the intense desire to catch up to her overrode my good sense.

As I approached, my van straining at the limits of metallic adhesion, she looked at me in her mirror, then sped up, staying just ahead of me.

This was a gutsy girl, but what was she up to? Then I saw that she was talking on a car phone, and I realized what she was doing. I backed off the gas, but it was too late. A black-and-white appeared in my mirror as Trish peeled off onto a side street and accelerated.

A second police cruiser fell in behind the first, and I knew what they were planning. Sure enough, their overhead lights came on.

I pulled over immediately and kept my hands on the steering wheel. Trish had called the cops on me. But why? Sure, I was following her, but she could have gotten away easily. I wasn't a stranger, and I had tried to talk to her at the door first. Why hadn't she called the cops from the house?

Did she think I was the one who killed Everett? If so, then there was no doubt she knew why he was killed. But did she know who?

I was in for another surprise. The police weren't moving up to talk to me. In the mirrors I could see they were hunkered down behind their doors, their guns leveled in my direction. They were following felony car stop procedure, a routine I knew well. If I didn't do exactly what they said, I was in for a world of hurt. And to make it worse, these guys were all new to the department and didn't know me.

Cautiously, I rolled the window down so I could hear their commands.

"Driver! With your left hand throw out the keys!"

I did it.

"With your right hand reach out and open the door, then get out slowly with both hands raised!"

I complied.

"With your arms up, turn around completely one time!"

They were seeing if I had weapons stuck in my waistband. I stopped when I was facing them, although I knew what was next.

"Now turn so that you're facing away from us!"

When my back was to them, I stopped.

"Back up slowly towards me, keep your hands up!"

As I passed between the front fenders of the side-by-side police cars I was told to get down on my knees and put my hands behind my head, fingers interlaced, and cross my ankles. Yeah, these were rookies. They were doing everything right, just like they learned in the academy. Veteran officers would have yanked me out through the window, twisted my arms off and beaten me with them, then taken my name.

As soon as I was in position, someone came up and cuffed me. A gun was being held very close to my head. I couldn't see it, but I could smell the gun oil. A veteran's gun would have smelled of dust and cobwebs.

I was checked for weapons and jerked to a standing position. Now was my chance to talk.

"My I.D.'s in my right rear pocket. Call Leitenant Brown, he knows me."

The officer retrieved my I.D. and saw my park security photo card. "So Brown knows you. So what? He knows a lot of crooks."

"I'm assisting him on the Curran case. I'm an ex-cop."

"Get fired?" His tone was sarcastic. And typical. I knew what was coming next. "From cop to security guard. Not what you call moving up."

I steeled myself against the insult. "All you have to do is call him."

"He's a busy man, buster. How about if I call the chief instead?"

"Okay," I said. He jerked on my cuffs as he guided me toward the rear door of his car. "Ow!" It was time to play hardball.

"What am I charged with?"

"Stalking."

"That's a misdemeanor. Where's your victim?"

"Shut up, pal." The standard comeback when you don't have a legitimate one.

"A misdemeanor not committed in your presence requires a citizen's arrest. All you have me for is driving up the street. Without a victim you have no probable cause and can't arrest me without a warrant because it's not a felony."

"All right, F. Lee Bailey, try this one on: suspicion of murder."

"Let's see," I baited. "False arrest—ow!" He had intentionally tightened the cuffs. "And brutality! And violation of my civil rights. Who can I get to help me spend the money—?"

He stuffed me, not too gently, into the back seat of his patrol car. A tow truck arrived to hook my van. We were both taken away, only to different places.

Yeah, maybe I'd earned the treatment. But I was right, in every detail. If I wasn't, I wouldn't have said anything. My problem has always been verbalizing my rightness to everyone around me, be they peer or supervisor. People hate it when I'm right, but they hate *me* when I point it out. I chastised myself for my big mouth.

At the station I was hustled into a cell, bypassing the booking cage, and left alone, unprocessed, for a half-hour or so. No phone calls, no charges. They hadn't filled out a booking sheet or taken my fingerprints or photograph. Good thing. I looked terrible.

The cell was small with painted cinder block walls and a bare concrete floor, yet, somehow, the faint odor of stale alcohol, B.O., urine, and antiseptic spray lingered. My eyes burned a little and not from fatigue. Someone had been sprayed with mace in here recently, a violation of department policy, but probably necessary.

I sat on the edge of a mattress that rested on top of a steel platform they called a bed, then yielded to my fatigue and leaned back into the corner, my feet up on the lip of the steel bunk, my forearms resting on my knees. My heavy eyelids drooped, and without some activity to keep me going, I quickly drifted off. This was the same cell I had placed a particularly pesky serial killer in following that sixty-two hour marathon, and as I wafted off into an uneasy sleep, I thought of him.

He wasn't as notorious as a Jeffrey Dahmer or a Ted Bundy or a John Wayne Gacy, although he could have been. Fortunately, we got to him before he went quite that far. He would have kept killing. They all do. Nothing stops a serial killer except incarceration or death. This one was a classic, an organized type, who maintained his pattern so carefully that he was relatively easy to predict, within certain limits. He even wanted to be stopped, so he left us intentional clues—on top of a myriad of unintentional ones—and wrote messages in his victim's blood, challenging us, and, at the same time, begging us to stop him.

And stop him we did, Theo and I, but not before three young women had been murdered: all with curly brown hair, all abducted from mall parking lots, and all over five-foot-five. He fit the profile we had developed so closely, it gave us chills.

He was quite helpful once we'd captured him, showing us where he buried all the body parts. Well, most of them. Certain internal organs he was unable to locate.

I was jarred by the sound of the big brass key being inserted into the lock on the heavy steel door. It opened slowly and a grim-faced Lieutenant Brown walked in, followed by the smirking officer that had arrested me.

"Here you go, hot shot," the rookie said. "Your best friend, Lieutenant Brown."

I leaned back against the wall. "Hello, Theo."

Theo turned to the officer. "Officer Collins, do me a favor. Go to the hallway where all the plaques and awards are, look at the pictures and read every plaque. Thumb through the department scrap book. If you don't find this man's name or picture ten times, you're off the hook. But you're in it deep, because it'll be there at least twenty times, sometimes alongside mine. When you're done there, I want a memo explaining why I wasn't called when a citizen requested you to call me. Especially an ex-cop. Do you have any idea what kind of trouble you're in? And not just with me, but with the Justice Department? The way you explained it, all the girl said was she was being followed, that someone was bothering her. That's all you had, her statement over the phone. You didn't even have dispatch tell her to hang around, identify him, and sign a complaint. Where is she? Can you substantiate her story? What if she was making it up? I don't believe you can prove that this man has committed any crime. The person we wanted was the girl. She's a material witness in a homicide case. Did you sleep through the academy?"

I had to turn away so the blue suit couldn't see me smiling. I actually believed he was getting smaller. Theo was laying it on thick and started to back him out the door as his harangue continued.

In a few minutes he booted the youngster out. I almost felt sorry for the guy. Almost.

Theo came back to the cell.

"Bravo," I said. "Now let me out."

Theo brought a chair into the cell and locked himself in.

"We've been having some trouble with that one," he said matter-of-factly. "If my little tirade doesn't change him, he'll never pass probation. He's got some good skills, but he's a little badge heavy. And no common sense."

"And he's rude. Now open the door."

"So what were you doing to get yourself arrested?"

"I was trying to talk to Trish Smith, of course."

"Why?"

"Oh, come on, Theo. Just a few hours ago you told me to find out what I could."

"I also told you to keep me posted."

"Unlike the girl, I don't have a car phone. And my Dick

Tracy two-way wrist radio is in for repairs. Besides, I haven't found anything out yet."

"Why were you chasing her?"

"Theo, I drive an old, heavy, six-cylinder van. She was driving a BMW and had a head start. Now you tell me: Was I chasing her?"

"She didn't want to talk to you."

"That much I know."

"Why do you suppose that is?"

"Because she doesn't know who I am. All she knows is someone from the park killed Everett, and from her point of view, it might be me."

"From my point of view, it doesn't look much different."

"What?"

"You found the kid. He should have gone undetected for several more hours, maybe longer. Just lucky, huh? From what I understand, you weren't supposed to be inside that ride. Best way I know to point attention away from yourself is to be a witness. Nobody has a motive, so you're even with everyone in that regard. On top of all that, you're caught chasing the dead kid's girlfriend. I'd say you're the prime suspect."

Now I was genuinely scared. Everything Theo said was true. I hadn't thought of it before—probably because I knew I hadn't done it—but I realized I could be made to look pretty bad.

"Are you really entertaining that idea, Theo?"

He gave me a hard look out of the corner of his eye, then relaxed his stare. "No. But I just came from a meeting with my captain, your senior vice president, and Harry Clark."

"And they think I did it?"

"It's an avenue I should pursue, I was told."

"Harry said that? What does he know about it? And since when—"

"No, the captain said it after Hayes and Clark left. They were just pressing for a quick resolution."

"Captain Fitzgerald?"

"You got it."

William J. "Don't Call Me Bill" Fitzgerald. A pompous, self-educated idiot. A fifteen-year veteran who had only one year of experience . . . fifteen times. He was so good at pushing papers around that he rose quickly in the department according to the Peter Principle: in a hierarchy some people tend to rise to the level of their incompetence. He was an adequate patrolman but had no people skills and should never have been a supervisor because his judgment was questionable. He was so full of himself and his self-perceived word power that his reports were filled with big words and flowery sentences, and so packed with irrelevant details as to make them incomprehensible. Somehow, in a bizarre twist of fate, he made sergeant when there was no one else to challenge him for the position.

To cover their mistake, the administration removed him from line supervision, giving him an administrative assistant spot, and soon he was promoted, again being in the right place at the right time. Nearly a decade went by, and, suddenly, because of a change of chiefs, he was squeezed up to captain, like a sliver that finally festers and pops out.

Most of us thought he had a drinking problem. He had wine with every meal, drank beer all day on weekends, and frequently came in late with puffy red eyes, but the administration turned a blind eye to it. Why they did so, we couldn't figure out.

"He's never liked me," I reminded Theo. "You know that."

"There was absolute delight in his voice and a sparkle in his eye when your name came up."

"I'll bet."

"What'd you ever do to him, anyway?"

"I have no idea, Theo. That's the funny part. He's always hated me, and I have no idea why."

"Ever ask him?"

"C'mon, you know Fitzgerald. He wouldn't admit it."

"Probably not. You know, Gil, he's always seen you as a threat to him."

"Only in his mind."

Theo shrugged. "Maybe. But how do you change people's perceptions?"

"If I knew, I'd do it. I made a conscious effort never to give him any reason to see me that way."

"Yeah, I know," Theo said. "But weak, paranoid, ineffective people are just naturally threatened by people like you."

"What's that supposed to mean?"

"A compliment, I assure you. You knew what you were doing, did a heck of a good job and didn't need supervision."

I waved him off. "I just did what I had to, what the job called for."

"True, but maybe you weren't humble enough."

Puzzled, I looked up at him. "I don't remember gloating or going around congratulating myself."

"No, it's just the way you . . . the way you carried yourself. It seemed . . . arrogant at times. That's why Fitzgerald is so pleased you're a lowly security guard."

"There's a difference between confidence and arrogance. Besides, I'm not a lowly security guard—"

Theo held up his hand. "His attitude, not mine."

I put my feet on the floor and fell silent for a moment, thinking about what he'd said. But I was too tired to go any deeper into the subject. I looked up.

"Listen, Theo, are you going to let me out of here?"

"Oh, yeah." He got up and unlocked the door. "Do yourself a favor," he said as I stepped out.

I looked at him with one eyebrow raised. "What?"

"Let me handle the rest of this investigation. If you keep trying to see people, it's going to look bad for you."

"I haven't done anything wrong. I've still got some things to follow up on."

"Leave the girl to me."

I shrugged, too tired to argue. "Whatever you say, Theo."

He walked me through the department, taking me to the front desk so I could get a release for my van. Several of my buddies from my glory days saw me, and the reunions slowed the trip considerably, although they lifted my spirits.

I had to admit it, I missed this place.

"What about Curran's autopsy?" I asked Theo when we were alone again and nearing our destination.

He stopped walking. "Pretty much confirmed what you thought. Solid blow to the head, most likely two. The first one was enough, though. Shattered the skull at the hat line in back, depressed it a good inch into the brain. Whoever did it was real strong or real mad.

"I vote for strong. Anger doesn't seem to be a part of this."

"I agree," Theo said.

"Any other trauma?" I asked. "Any signs of a struggle?"

"No bruises, cuts, anything. No signs of any struggle anywhere. No defensive wounds on the hands. He was like a lamb led to slaughter."

"Do you think he was aware it was coming?"

Theo shook his head slowly. "My guess is they were talking to him and someone cold-cocked him from behind. Probably never knew what hit him."

"So there had to be two people."

"At least. Unless a single killer was somehow able to distract Curran into turning his back, then picked up the rod without the boy noticing and clubbed him."

"I doubt it," I said. "And I don't think there would have been more than two people there. Don't ask me why, that's just a gut feeling I have. And the two people that were there, Everett knew them and trusted them."

"Looks that way," Theo agreed. "But that doesn't bring us any closer to finding out who they are."

"At least we can reduce the possible suspect list. We're looking for a strong, cold-blooded person with a reason to kill a harmless kid."

"Whom Everett knew and trusted."

"Who had access to the park at night."

"And a key to the rides."

"If it was locked," I added.

Theo raised an eyebrow. "Aren't they kept secured?"

"Usually. But accidents happen, just like in the real world. Besides, a key wouldn't be that hard to come by if someone really wanted it." A realization struck me. "You know, Theo, I just remembered. The back door and shop doors are kept locked. But if you walk up to the loading dock, you can follow the tracks right into the tunnel. The only thing you'd have to have is a flashlight to keep from tripping over the rails."

Theo took that information and chewed on it, then shrugged. "We're right back where we started."

"Not necessarily," I said. "We still have the motive angle. I suspect a strong one in this case, one that's bound to surface sooner or later."

"If no one else gets hurt in the meantime." We both knew that the first forty-eight hours after a murder were the most important. After that, solving the crime gets increasingly tougher. It struck me that perhaps that was another reason I was so interested in foregoing sleep to decipher this mystery.

Theo moved on again, his mood a bit more sullen than before, and I followed. He took me into the lobby and reached through the reception window, coming out with a slip of paper which he handed to me. I thought I detected the flicker of a smile across his face, but it faded quickly and I couldn't be sure. I looked at the paper, a release for my van, and knew it had indeed been a look of satisfied amusement.

"Hey!" I said. "Sixty-five dollars for the tow bill? You don't expect me to pay for that rookie's fiasco, do you?"

Theo just smiled and headed back toward the door to the interior hallway.

"Have a nice day," he said as he disappeared inside.

My trump card hadn't been played yet. Would ol' Bill Fitzgerald swap sixty-five bucks for a promise not to sue for false arrest?

EIGHT

After retrieving my precious van, I sat in it in a restaurant parking lot, tired and dejected. I had spent most of the day—when I should have been sleeping—trying to find and talk to one little blonde girl. Not only did I fail, it cost me sixty-five bucks, and I ended up becoming the prime suspect.

It had not been a good day.

And yet . . . something about the way Trish reacted was encouraging. I was on the right trail. She suspected a park employee, and not just any old employee, either. Someone who could have an accomplice in security.

Or anybody with fake I.D. No, I was jumping to conclusions. All I really knew was that she suspected a park employee, just as the police and I did. But she also felt she was in danger for the same reason Everett was killed. I had to believe she knew what it was.

I dragged myself into the restaurant. Hollie was at the register and watched me walk in.

"You look terrible!" she said.

"Thank you," I said, meaning it. I felt worse than terrible.

"I thought I told you to get some sleep."

"Yeah, well, I had things to do."

"I think you'd be better off with a few hours sleep than a greasy dinner."

"Are you saying the food in here is greasy?" I asked accusingly.

She smiled. "That's what makes it good. But you need some sleep."

"Thank you, Mother, I know. I've already been told."

"Suit yourself, Superman. I'm just trying to help."

"First eat, then sleep," I concluded. She shrugged and gave up on me. Patting my arm, she showed me to my booth, took my order, and left.

I ate without enjoying it and drank lots of coffee. Not that it helped. Caffeine never had much effect on me. It was more to have something to do. And I don't remember what I ate, except that it was greasy and good.

I didn't even try to figure anything out, to put together what few pieces of the puzzle I had. I was too exhausted, and my mind too muddied to make any sense of the whole thing.

With the restriction Theo had placed on me, there wasn't much else I could do. His captain was putting pressure on him to keep me out of it. Fitzgerald knew I hadn't killed the kid. He just wanted Theo to think twice about soliciting—or even accepting—my help. Fitzgerald couldn't stand to let someone else get the credit for anything. He had to be in complete control. The idea of an outsider working on the case—especially this outsider—prompted Fitzgerald to tighten the reins on Theo.

That settled it. I was going to solve this. I'd go home and get some sleep—I had to be back to work in six hours—but I wanted to do one more thing first.

After paying for my dinner, I climbed into the behemoth and set a course for the Curran house. Maybe there was something there that would explain why he was killed.

I knew Theo and his men had already been there, but maybe they missed something. You could never tell. They were on a little different wavelength than me.

Returning to the house I had driven past earlier, I parked out front. Both Delta 88s were still in the driveway. I walked slowly up to the front porch and knocked on the white-painted door with the decorative and functional brass knocker.

The door was opened by a tired-looking woman, her hair mussed, dress wrinkled, and eyes swollen and red from crying. She was not crying now, but appeared exhausted, almost sick from doing it. She had aged well and didn't appear much over her mid-forties, maybe fifty. Her hair had a smattering of gray and was nicely styled, although it had not been attended to today for obvious reasons. She wore an apron over a cotton print dress, lacking in style but utilitarian and undoubtedly comfortable.

"Mrs. Curran?"

"Yes?" Her tone was apprehensive, as if she was saying *now what?* I wondered how many people had come by today.

I introduced myself. "I'm really sorry to bother you Mrs. Curran, but I was wondering if I could have a word with you. I know it's not a good time, but it's really important."

She just stood there, not knowing what to do and too tired to think.

"Mrs. Curran, I was the one who discovered Everett's . . . uh, your son this morning."

"Oh." A flicker of pain creased her face, and she backed up, opening the door wide for me to enter.

The interior of the house was as I expected: tastefully furnished in early American discount, with lots of knitted Afghans covering the chairs and hand-made knick-knacks all over the place. Family photos covered the top of the console television. There were several of Everett at all ages, alone and with another boy who was at least six or seven years older. And a recent picture of Trish, probably her senior photo from high school judging by the hair and pose.

In the adjoining dining room, the walls were covered by a reproduction of DaVinci's *Last Supper* and two collection cabinets, one of spoons and one of thimbles.

The place reminded me of my own home growing up. It had the same comfortable feel, warm brown colors, and casual furniture that I was actually allowed to sit on. We didn't have a family room. The living room was it, and we spent most of our family time in there, or in the kitchen. Company was treated like family, not "entertained" in a formal room. School projects were spread out on the chrome and green Formica kitchen table. Plastic models were built on newspapers and then cleared off for meals. There was always a jar of cookies, usually chocolate chip, sometimes peanut butter.

Slipcovers protected our furniture. We had the same sofa for as long as I could remember, and it never showed any wear, as I recall. My parents finally had it reupholstered about five years after I moved out. We still had it when my mom died. Dad died on the sofa watching a ball game. It was the only couch they ever owned.

I would not have been surprised to see a jigsaw puzzle in progress on the Curran's dining room table. I imagined them plugging in a few pieces every night after dinner, and, upon completing it, taking a snapshot, then scooping it back into the box and starting over with another five hundred piece view of dramatic American landscape.

Mrs. Curran motioned for me to sit in an upholstered chair by the unlit fireplace. As I settled into my seat, a man I presumed to be Everett's father came in from the kitchen, wiping his hands with a towel. He was dressed in garage clothes, the kind of thing my dad used to wear when he worked in the garage on Saturdays. The sleeves of his flannel shirt were rolled up. He wore bifocals, and his full head of hair was dark except for a small brush of gray on the sides.

"Estelle, I put the—Oh, I'm sorry. I didn't know we had company."

I stood and Mrs. Curran introduced me to her husband. As I shook his hand she added, "He's the man who found Everett."

"Oh . . . please sit down." The same look of pain furrowed his brow.

"Thank you," I said. "I know this is a bad time for you, but I wanted to tell you how sorry I am."

"Did you know Everett?" Mr. Curran asked.

"No, not really. I work at night." Mrs. Curran wasn't listening. She had started to cry again. Her husband looked puzzled, as if to ask *then why are you here?* But he didn't say anything.

I happened to notice on the wall by the fireplace a picture of Jesus: the familiar one that is so famous. Although there is no passage in the Bible that describes His features, we know He was a Jew, a carpenter, and carried the weight of the world on His shoulders. We also know that Isaiah referred to Him as having no form or comeliness, and that when we see Him, there is no beauty that we should desire Him. Somehow I don't think that picture is even close to what he looked like.

But we all know who the picture represents, and its place of prominence on the Curran's wall assured me that Theo's information was accurate. The large family Bible on the coffee was a King James, opened to John's Gospel. A small bookshelf nearby held familiar titles that I had often seen in the local Christian bookstore, and I noticed the little angel children figurines on the mantle.

Their grief was understandable and obvious, but they were holding up remarkably well. Life was continuing for them, and I attributed their stalwart perseverance to the faith I presumed they had.

I leaned forward and spoke quietly. "I don't know if this will be much comfort to you, but I'm sure God has a reason for all this."

Mrs. Curran wiped her cheek with a tissue and spoke through sniffles. "You believe in God?"

"Yes, ma'am. I'm a Christian."

"Oh, that's good to hear."

"Mrs. Curran, I've seen many things like this that I don't understand. Never will understand. I don't mean to get too theological here, but I heard in my Sunday morning Bible study not too long ago an interesting perspective on why bad things happen to good people. Because of sin, we all deserve to die. That fact that most of us don't is evidence of God's mercy. I know that God loves His children. And God knew what He was doing when He allowed this to happen to Everett. There's a purpose in it."

"I know," she said, "I know. But Everett was such a good boy. Why him?"

"Mrs. Curran, we live in a fallen world. We breathe polluted air. We get in car wrecks. We lose jobs. We grow old, get sick—-just like everyone else. The difference is, we have a Savior who comforts us when times are bad, when we are hurting. And who is waiting for us when it's our time to go and be with Him."

"He's right, honey," Mr. Curran said. "Everett's with Jesus now. We're not crying for him, but us. We'll get through this, Estelle."

She nodded, unable to speak.

"Trials break our sense of sovereignty over our lives," I said softly, "to drive us to Him, and to each other. It's something I am still learning."

Mrs. Curran smiled at me weakly through her tears. I could see her chest jerk as she spasmed, fighting back more anguish. I was about to break down, too.

My mind flickered back to a scene from my past, although I didn't know why at the time. But I went with it, seeing a cute teenage girl gazing up at me as I pinned a corsage on her prom dress with shaking hands. Her auburn hair was piled high on her head, and her face, free of all but the slightest hint of makeup, glowed. I should have been aware that it was because of me, but my ego was so insecure back then that I thought she was just happy to get out of the house for the night.

In retrospect, that was ridiculous. Rachel got along with her parents okay, and they stood in the background in my mind movie, arms around each other, grinning, watching their little girl go off on a serious date with a stuttering, straight-A geek who was interested in reading *Lord of the Rings* and mystery novels and was clueless about what he was going to major in once he got to college. I would go. There was no question about that. My parents had been emphatic, despite the financial burden it would be. But on that night I had no real direction.

Rachel would change that for me. Her prom dress transformed into a nice Easter Sunday outfit without the hat, and she aged about seven years. Still she beamed, watching her husband, a college grad with a degree in administration of justice, a graduate from the police academy in a crisp, navy blue, class A uniform. The stutter was gone, replaced by a confident swagger in his step. Her hair was down now in a style worn by many of the teachers in her elementary school. She planned to get a few more years experience under her belt, then sign on with a Christian school where she could also teach the children about Jesus, the source of all knowledge and truth.

Which brought me to the final scene, the one that was burning inside me now, stirred by the Currans' grief for their boy.

"Mrs. Curran." I stopped to swallow. "I'm a widower. My wife was a schoolteacher. She was thirty-five when she collapsed one morning in her classroom just before the kids came in. The principal and then the paramedics tried . . ." I coughed to cover up my own heartache. "They tried to bring her back, but nothing worked. When they did the autopsy they couldn't find anything wrong. Her heart, brain, lungs, everything was normal." The tears came, unstoppable now. I was too tired and spent to fight them back.

"They couldn't find a physical reason for her death. It remains a mystery. All I could do was assume God needed her with Him, to teach . . . all the little children in heaven."

"Oh, I'm so sorry," Mrs. Curran said, crying in sympathy with me. "Do you have any children?"

"No ma'am."

She got up and walked over to me, gave me a big hug, and wiped my tears with a tissue.

"In a way that's too bad," she said. "Then you'd have someone to hug, someone who'd remind you of your precious wife. But in another sense, it's good. The children would have so much pain to deal with for their whole life. And you'd feel their pain with them in addition to your own. Like you said, God knows what He's doing."

"You know," I said slowly, examining my hands, "for a long time I've wondered about it. I mean, I know God is in control, and I trust Him, but, in spite of what I know to be true about trials, there are times when I can't help but wonder, why. Why take her? What is there for me to accomplish that losing her would somehow make possible? What am I to learn from this? Please, don't misunderstand. I'm not challenging God. I'm not even questioning Him, not in the fist-shaking sense. It's just . . . will I ever know?"

"Perhaps," Mrs. Curran said, patting my hand. "And perhaps not. Now, I'm sure you know this, but I'm going to say it anyway. We all need to be reminded now and then. There's two things you need to do when you are bothered by this. Praise God for who He is, and ask Him to give you wisdom. Not the answer to your question, but wisdom and guidance. Then, just go about your business. Keep Him first, He'll fill in the blanks."

I smiled. She was right. And I was pretty good about doing it, except when my memory was scratched and new blood drawn as it had been when I entered the Curran house. And now, here they were, the grieving parents, comforting a crusty, cynical, leather-skinned ex-cop. It was funny in a strange, wonderful sort of way, how one minute I was answering her questions and counseling her in her grief, and the next minute she was doing the same for me. Those of us in the body of Christ really do need each other.

"Thank you," I said, sniffing. "Is that another son?" I nodded toward the photos on the television.

"Yes. That's Everett's older brother, Randolph. He's married and living in the Sierra-Nevadas."

Mr. Curran picked up the narrative. "Runs a fishing resort on June Lake. You like to fish?"

I nodded. "Very much, but I don't get many chances to go."

"Maybe you can find some time soon. I'll take you there. It'll be good for both of us."

"Sounds good." I wondered what was going through his mind. Does he need a replacement son, or did Everett not like to fish? Either way, I thought he was right. It would do us both good.

We all fell silent for a moment. Words seemed empty somehow. I took a deep breath, remembering why I was there and how tired I was, and decided to get back to business and plunge ahead with my request.

"Folks, let me explain why I'm here, other than to tell you how sorry I am. I'm trying to find out who did this. I work for the park now but used to be with the police department. Has Lt. Theo Brown been here?"

Mrs. Curran nodded slowly while Mr. Curran said, "Yes, early this morning."

"I used to work with Lietenant Brown. I know a lot about the park that might help us find out who did this to your son. I was wondering if you'd mind if I took a look in his room."

"What are you looking for?"

"Anything that might give me a clue why this happened, and who did it."

"The police already went through his room."

"I'm sure they did. And I don't question their ability. But I know more about the park than they do. Something that didn't mean anything to the police might mean something to me."

Mr. Curran's brow furrowed. "Are you saying that someone who works with Ev killed him?" Mrs. Curran looked up, shocked, and put her hand over her mouth.

"That seems likely," I admitted.

"It's okay with me, if it'll help. Estelle?" He looked at his wife.

She looked lost, helpless, pleading for relief from this insanity. She did not answer.

"Go ahead," Mr. Curran told me quietly. "It's through that door, down the hall to the last door on the right."

"Thank you," I said, rising. "I won't be long."

He nodded once and turned his attention back to his grieving wife.

As I left the living room, I remembered what it was I hated about being a cop.

NINE

I opened the door expectantly, thinking I'd find a typical room: messy, posters on the wall, clothes all over the floor. But it wasn't that way. The room was neat, clothes were hung up, no rock posters—although there were a few pieces of artwork adorning the walls: cartoons, surreal landscapes, sci-fi monsters and spacecraft.

The bed was made. Considering that it had only been fifteen hours or so since I found his body, and Mrs. Curran was too upset to have cleaned up his room, and I doubted that Theo had made the bed, I figured Everett was not only a neat, tidy young man, but he also hadn't slept in the bed at all last night.

Wait a minute! His car had been parked so far out in the employee lot because—at the time he parked it—that was the closest space! He had arrived at the park when it was still open, and there were still hundreds of employee's vehicles filling the lot. That's why he hadn't slept in the bed. He was somewhere in the park all evening until he was murdered. Chances are whoever he was with killed him, or knew who did. Surely someone saw them together. It would be a monumental task, but everyone who worked that day would have to be interviewed. I made a mental note to check Everett's work schedule to see if he had been there during the day at all.

In the corner of the room was a drawing table. All Everett's drawing supplies—the pencils, ink pens, color markers and such—were neatly arranged in special holders next to the table. The table itself was clear.

So, he's an artist. I remembered the pictures on the wall and turned to inspect them closely. They were originals, not prints, drawn very carefully and in great detail. In the corner of each was his signature, with the exception of a dramatic scene of a tyrannosaur locked in mortal combat with a triceratops. It was unsigned.

The shelf at one end of the room held a fascinating array of knick-knacks. There were brass antique automobiles about two inches long, small plastic dinosaurs, a pocketwatch inside a glass dome, and figurines of people from different eras such as cowboys, knights in armor, cavemen, and Roman soldiers.

Next to the drawing table was a computer kept dust-free with plastic covers. The computer had a barrel-key lock, and it was in the locked position.

As I turned to leave, disappointed at not finding anything obvious, I noticed a two-drawer metal file cabinet in a recessed area behind the door. It, too, was locked, as I expected, although there appeared to be small pry marks in the gap between the drawer and the side of the cabinet near the locking mechanism. Perhaps Everett had misplaced his key once.

If I was going to look in that file cabinet, I would need the key. I walked out and found Mr. Curran alone in the living room.

"Mr. Curran?"

He looked up. "Did you find anything?"

"Not yet. Do you know where Everett kept the keys to his file cabinet?"

"You think there's something in there that can help you?"

"Don't know. That'd be the best place, I'd think."

"Well, he's pretty organized. Was, I should say. Boy, that's going to be hard getting used to."

"Yes sir. Uh, about the key . . . ."

"Don't know. We respect each other's privacy in this house, and I never needed to know where he kept his keys. You know, you look awful tired."

"I was up all last night, and I haven't been to bed yet."

"You stayed up trying to solve this?"

"Yes sir."

"Why don't you go get some sleep? You can come back tomorrow."

"If it's all the same to you, I'd like to keep going. Once I find the keys it will only take me a few minutes."

"Suit yourself, but I can't help you with the keys."

I returned to Everett's room and looked around. If I were Everett, where would I hide my keys? If it were *me,* they'd be in my pocket. No, I think Everett would put them someplace neat and logical. I started opening everything that would open: drawers, jewelry chests, underneath some of the curious knick-knacks on the shelf.

After a few futile minutes Mrs. Curran came in to find me standing in the middle of the room and rubbing my jaw.

"Harold just told me what you needed." She walked over to the closet and opened it. I was amused—and relieved—to discover why Everett's room was so neat. Like every other kid and bachelor in the world, it all went into the closet.

Mrs. Curran pulled out a hanger holding a dark blue blazer with a coat-of-arms on the pocket. "Everett hates this jacket." She reached into the pocket and pulled out a key ring.

"I'm a mother," she explained with a anguished expression as she handed the keys to me. Although I hadn't asked, she obviously felt the need to explain. "I never looked for his keys before. But once when I suggested giving the jacket to the needy, he just about had a fit. When I thought about it just now . . . ." She trailed off. "If you'll excuse me . . . ." She hurried out.

I waited a second, then unlocked the file cabinet. The top drawer was only partly filled. Manila folders were duly marked according to their contents: Car, Stereo, Work, School, Trish

. . . *Trish?* I had to look. There were cards, a few letters, a napkin, ticket stubs. Good for you, Everett. Everyone was wrong. He knew exactly how she felt about him, and he felt the same way about her. I didn't read the letters, but closed the folder reverently.

Most of the files contained important papers such as receipts, repair bills, warranty papers. I opened the WORK folder hoping to find something of interest. Instead, I was disappointed. All it contained was a photocopy of his application, a memo from his shift supervisor about his request for assignment change (denied), and his last performance evaluation.

I scanned this document. He was rated average, largely because of his lack of enthusiasm. Someone, probably Everett, had written something across the bottom. I tried to make out the handwriting. "Insignificant" it looked like. I wondered what that meant. I replaced the file.

The bottom drawer was full, mostly with artwork. Sketches of all kinds and mediums and subjects. There were portraits, charcoals, cartoons, crayon landscapes, pen and ink drawings, watercolors . . . .Everett Curran was a fantastic artist. Because of his age, I figured him to be largely untrained, at least formally. Maybe he had taken a class or two, but for the most part he appeared to have natural, God-given talent. In spite of myself, and in spite of knowing better, I couldn't help but ask, *Why, God?* So talented, yet, taken away in his prime.

There were many pictures of dinosaurs, and some of them had a familiar look to them. I puzzled over these briefly, only understanding when I came across one that also had a gondola in it. A park gondola, shaped like a broken dinosaur egg. These were drawings of the park's dinosaur kingdom ride.

And yet, there was something different about it. There were details the actual ride lacked. Apparently Everett had some ideas for improving the ride. I wondered if he had ever submitted them. I made a note to myself to ask.

In addition to the dinosaurs, there were other concept drawings. Space platforms, capsules, highly-detailed alien creatures, wild west towns, cowboys and gamblers and gunfighters, events out of history both known and imagined. At least, I didn't recognize them. Then there was a stack of cartoons, comic strips like in the newspaper, all starring a little talking dinosaur, as well as model sheets for the dinosaur character in all kinds of costumes and situations.

At the back of the drawer was a file marked PROJECT. It was empty. I closed the drawer, thought for a minute, then reopened the top drawer and returned to the TRISH file. Maybe I could find a clue that would help me locate her. If she was in fear, she'd be foolish to stay home. If the BMW was any indication, she probably had access to enough money to stay at a motel for awhile, or maybe with relatives. No, she probably wanted to be alone. I would. But where would she go? She couldn't sit around in a motel room all day. That'd drive her nuts. She'd need to occupy her mind, find something to do.

She'd want to remember, reminisce. She'd go someplace they had gone together, someplace special.

I scanned the letters, feeling guilty about it but feeling also it was a necessity. There was no talk about love, no revelations about their deep feelings, only chit-chat about *how are you? Did you enjoy the church social?* kind of stuff. Nothing that looked important as far as his murder was concerned. As I started to replace the folder, though, I caught a glimpse of something below the hanging folders in the bottom of the drawer.

It was a ticket stub from the Skateaway, an ice rink at a nearby mall. My guess was it meant something special to him, probably to her, too. It was obvious to me why it was important.

They had touched. Held hands.

Standard operating procedure at a skate rink. Even Everett would've done that, no matter how shy he might have been. Especially if he couldn't skate very well.

And to a kid like Everett—straight-laced, sensitive—the touch of Trish's hand would be monumental.

Would she go there to mourn? I made a mental note to check, but it would have to wait until tomorrow.

I put the stub in my pocket, angry now at the killer for what he had done to her, too.

Closing the drawer, I moved over to the computer. It was an older model with dual floppies and no hard drive. The monitor was obviously monochrome. Very slow, but functional. I was beginning to feel both frustrated by not finding anything and expectant that it had to be here. Curran was an outstanding artist. The park could have used him in Design and Planning. But, like so many others, Everett was assigned perfunctory chores that didn't tap into his talent and was then evaluated as average.

I looked again at the key ring. There was a small key next to the computer key. Probably for the disk file box. But there was no disk file box, something I found odd. I got down and put my eye at table top level and sighted down next to the computer where there was a small space. Sure enough, there was a rectangle that wasn't as dusty as the table top around it. There had been a disk file box here, but where was it now?

I had already searched the room and hadn't seen one. Could Theo have taken it? Probably. He would have thought the boy's personal artifacts interesting. I decided to ask him about it later.

But right now I wanted to look at his computer files. If Everett was like me—and in some respects he was—he'd have another copy of all his disks somewhere else—at least the important ones. Just in case.

Once again I surveyed the room. Where was a likely place? Someplace where the disks wouldn't be subject to extreme temperatures or bumps. Someplace padded . . . .

My eye lit on his dresser. The underwear drawer. Nobody went through an eighteen-year-old's underwear drawer, not even his mother if she knew what was good for her. It was as off-limits as a pit bull's mouth.

I opened the drawer slowly, half expecting something to

crawl out. Nothing did, and I tentatively pushed the jockey shorts aside.

There they were, safely protected in a plastic case. I freed the disks from their cotton and elastic dungeon, and closed the drawer quickly.

The diskette case opened with a plastic click. Inside were fifteen to twenty disks, each labeled in some fashion. I fingered through them. *Misc, History, Science, Music Apprec.* But just reading the labels was no clue as to what the disks really contained. I'd have to put them in my computer.

When I was running my business—the one I left the police department for—I acquired a little laptop computer. That was one of the few good decisions I had made. Fortunately Everett's disks were the right size, and my machine was compatible. I slipped the box in my pocket, took one final survey of the room, and returned to the living room.

The Currans were there, patiently waiting for me to complete my intrusive search. There was a temporary lull in their sorrow, probably brought on by fatigue and dehydration. But there would be more tears. There always would be more tears.

"Did you find anything?" Mr. Curran asked.

"Yes, sir. I don't know if it'll help any, but Everett had this box of computer disks. Do you have any idea what kind of projects he was working on?" Even as I asked the question, I realized how being tired had affected my ability to think clearly. I should have asked this question a long time ago. Mrs. Curran was his mother. She'd know!

But her answer surprised me.

"To be honest, we don't. He worked on so many things that we couldn't keep up. And he was so secretive about it. I think he didn't want to show us anything that wasn't perfect. He didn't take failure or criticism well."

I nodded. "I can understand that. Do you mind if I take these disks for a few days? I'll return them unharmed."

"I'm sure you will. I hope they help."

"Thank you. I best be going."

"Yes, you look tired."

I moved toward the door, then had a thought, one of many I should have had sooner.

"How well do you know Trish?"

"Oh, she's a doll! We think she really loves Everett, but they didn't date. She'll be crushed."

"Do you think she'll know what Everett was working on?"

"I'd say she'd be the only one," Mr. Curran said. Finally, I'd gotten something right.

"Do me a favor, please. If you talk to her, tell her I'm on her side. She's afraid of me, ran when I tried to talk to her. I believe she thinks I'm responsible or involved." I paused. "I think she could be the key to this, only she doesn't know it."

"Okay," Mr. Curran said. "We'll put in a good word for you."

"Thank you. Good-bye, and thanks for your help."

"Thank *you*."

"Yes, thank you," echoed Mrs. Curran. She came over to me and gave me a big, motherly hug. "And I'm sorry about your wife."

I nodded—it was all I could do—and left.

TEN

I drove home emotionally and physically exhausted. There was no more I could do today. I still had to work tonight and had only enough time for three or four hours sleep, at best. Earlier, when I had decided to stay up, I hadn't anticipated the events of the past hour.

Trish would just have to stay hidden for now. There are limits to everything, and I had reached mine. I prayed that God would protect her until I could find her. In the meantime, I had Everett's computer disks to go through.

The trip home was a nightmare. My head bobbed like one of those little dogs people put in their rear window, and I struggled to keep my eyes open. Several times I screamed at the top of my lungs to activate the adrenaline and even slapped myself in the face. It didn't work. Neither did hanging my head out the window. When I pulled into the driveway, not remembering most of the trip, it was all I could do to open the door, stagger in, and fall onto the bed fully-dressed.

When I woke to the alarm fifteen minutes later—the clock said three hours had passed, but I didn't believe it—I was still in the same position as when I had fallen asleep.

To save time, I put on a fresh uniform at home while a pot of coffee brewed. I poured this into a thermos, grabbed my laptop computer, and headed out. I had a long night ahead of me. In addition to my regular duties, I was going to try to go through the disks, if I had a chance, to see what was there.

I hoped Everett was as organized with his computer as he was everywhere else. The computer forced the issue, in part, requiring every file saved to have a name different from every other file. But those file names could be anything the user wanted. They didn't have to relate to the contents. They could be code names, abbreviations, cryptic anagrams, acrostics, whatever.

I stopped at the employee gate long enough to leave my laptop and thermos with Ralph—the disk case I kept in my jacket pocket—and made it to the time clock by the security office with only a few minutes to spare.

The guards rotated areas every night, and tonight I bartered for the backstage area. It wasn't my turn, but I promised the guy who had it that I'd buy him breakfast sometime. This area included all the office trailers, repair shops, warehouses, the design center, and other outbuildings that the public never saw. I would also cover the other guards' areas during their breaks. The backstage had the most walking but the least actual work and might give me the time I'd need.

Briefing was over quickly. Brito had little to say. I tried to slip out and start checking my area right away but was pigeonholed by several of the other guys—once we were out of Brito's sight—wanting to hear the gory details of the night before.

I gave them the Harry Clark version and hurried off to get my security checks over with quickly. The custodians were fairly predictable and, barring a painter or other specialized repairman that needed to be let in—they weren't allowed keys to offices or merchandise areas either—I'd get done soon enough to have some free time to do my own prowling.

When I spelled Ralph for his dinner, I set up my laptop on his desk and went to work reading the directories and file names on Everett's disks. There were the expected school related file names, like FRANKLIN, JEFFRSON, WAR1812, MONROEDC.

Perhaps I should explain to the non-users of computers that file names are limited to eight characters, plus an extension of up to three characters after a period if needed, such as WORLDHIS.101. Either the user modifies the spelling of his file name to limit it to eight, or the computer simply cuts it off after eight characters regardless of how many are typed in. Judging by the way the names were abbreviated, I figured Everett did it himself. I wasn't surprised.

These names were obviously history files. There was also an entire disk of files named TRISH, TRISH1, TRISH2, and so on. Probably letters to the love of his life, confirming that people were very wrong. Everett *had* noticed her and *did* feel more than just a friendship. Maybe he didn't let it show, but he felt it.

Why wouldn't he show it? Fear, maybe. Fear of rejection. Some women bring that out in a man. They're fine as long as you're a friend, but start to show a little intensity, and they get scared off. Maybe Everett was just unsure of himself. But if that were true, why would he send letters?

It struck me that maybe he hadn't sent them. He just wrote them, like a diary. I decided I wouldn't look at the letters but give them to Trish when the time was right. Although dead, Everett deserved some privacy. Let's face it, he'd already had a complete stranger exploring his room and the coroner exploring his body.

I continued going through the disks. Many of them were program disks with printed labels that I didn't need to check. I had a copy of his word processor which would make things easier when the time came, in case his files weren't compatible with mine. There were some games, including some of the more famous ones. No sports, I noticed. There were a few with handwritten labels, but I recognized the names. These were probably copies of programs he had gotten from someone else. One I wasn't familiar with—Space Tracer—I set aside, mildly curious. My small machine wouldn't run game programs that need a high-quality color monitor. I'd have to check that one somewhere else.

There were two more. One was labeled SUNSCHL, and when I read the directory, I understood. All the file names were Biblical. Everett even put his Sunday School notes into his computer.

The last disk—it's always the last one, isn't it?—had only about twenty files. The disk label had no name on it, just an X. One file was named RIDES, another COSTUMES, a third MERCH. I was beginning to get interested when I heard something behind me, some distance away; a shoe scuff on the pavement, rustling leaves. I hurriedly removed the disk and slipped them all into my coat pocket, shut down the machine and pushed it aside, then looked up, expecting to see Ralph.

There was no one in sight.

Puzzled at first, I figured it was probably just Sergeant Brito. He liked to sneak up on us and catch us goofing off, although he was never successful. Oh, we goofed off, don't get me wrong. He just never caught us.

In our defense, though, let me add that the work always got done, and the park was always secure. We did not neglect our responsibilities. Despite poor perimeter fencing, there were very few incidents over the years of unauthorized people getting inside the park. Those were mostly high school kids on a dare, not vandals.

Perhaps that's one reason I was so sure the killer was an employee and one authorized to be here at night. The question that raised was, how did *Everett* get in unobserved? The obvious assumption was, he didn't. He was already inside when the park closed.

But where? And why?

Ralph returned in a few minutes. I said nothing as I left, but when he sat down, he saw my note: *Brito is in bushes behind you.* He gave me two surreptitious clicks on his portable radio to let me know he understood. I smiled and made my way back to my area.

I opened a few doors for custodians, checked my area once, then gave Wendy her break. While I was in there, I learned that we'd hired a new guard. She'd shown up just a few minutes prior, and Brito was now giving her a tour of the park.

Wendy told me the new gal was an internal transfer from the Flapper Zone where she'd been an usher in the Bijou Theater. No previous experience in security. She'd start her formal training next week on graveyard.

"With who?" I asked Wendy.

"With whom."

"I asked you first."

"I was correcting your grammar."

"My grandma's deceased."

"Oh, stop it, Gil!"

"Sorry. It's just a frustrating habit I have."

"If you're frustrated with it, why don't you stop doing it?"

"I'm not frustrated with it. You are."

"You can say that again." She squeezed her eyes shut when she realized what she'd said.

I waited in silence.

"Well?" she asked finally.

"Well what?"

"Aren't you going to say it again?"

"Should I?"

"I thought you would."

"There you go, thinking again."

She walked back to her chair, shaking her head in disgust. But I knew, deep down inside, she really loved it.

"So, anyway," I asked, "are you going to answer my question?"

"What was it?"

"Whom's she training with?"

Wendy smiled a diabolical, in-your-face sort of smile. "With you, big guy. Serves you right."

I groaned, inwardly and outwardly. "Why me?"

"Because you're the best. Just ask you."

"Baloney. I never claimed that." I paused. "Have I?"

"No, you haven't. Not in so many words. But the way you carry yourself and play head games with people all the time, it's obvious you think it."

I was a little surprised. I hadn't realized my joking around had been mistaken for ego. And the way I carry myself? I don't float or strut, I just walk. Okay, so I'm confident in my abilities. Most of the time, anyway. Is that ego? What in the world did I do?

Apparently my thought showed on my face.

"Aw, don't worry about it, Gil," Wendy said. "I know you're okay. In fact, it's kind of entertaining the way you mix people up. I kind of enjoy it."

See, I told you.

"Thanks, Wendy. You're a good kid." I meant it in a complimentary way, and she knew it. "By the way, thanks for your help last night."

"Doing what?"

"Calling the cops. What in the world was Jaime thinking?"

"That you were playing one of your practical jokes. That's what he said as he walked out."

"I wouldn't joke about something like that. What if he *had* called the cops and I *was* joking? I'd have been in trouble!"

"I don't think he thought it through. He'd been trying to get a hold of you for fifteen minutes. He was already a little distracted. In fact, I'd say he was peeved. He'd broken a sweat worrying over you."

"Worry or anger?"

"Both, probably."

"Where is he now?"

"In the park somewhere, showing Mandy around."

"Mandy?"

"The new guard."

"What's she like?"

"Cute, thin, half your age."

"Ouch."

"Sorry, but it's true."

"Okay, fine, but that's not what I was getting at. I'm curious about why they hired someone like her to be a security guard."

Wendy gave me a perturbed look.

"Oh, yeah," I said. "Because it doesn't make sense, like everything else they do here. I should have known."

Wendy's radio crackled. It was Brito.

"Sam five to dispatch."

He was whispering.

"Sam five, go ahead," Wendy answered.

"Sam five, I'm in Camp Wilderness. There's a trespasser in the wheelhouse of the paddlewheel riverboat on Lake of Lights!"

"Ten-four." Wendy looked up at me, puzzled.

"I know what you're thinking," I said. "And you're right. Tell him back-up is rolling from the station."

Wendy smiled and repeated what I told her to Brito.

"Okay," Brito said.

"How long has he worked here?" I asked.

"Long enough," was Wendy's reply.

I hurried out toward the interior of the amusement park collecting a couple of the other guys to go with me. I wanted witnesses. As we drew near, we put in our earphones so our radios wouldn't be heard and snuck up to the scene through the bushes, stopping under cover when we were close enough to see Brito and Mandy.

He was hunkered down by the side of the boat with Mandy crouching behind him, shaking visibly. There was room for three more of her there, and all of them would be completely protected. I snickered at the sight. If Brito lost his balance, she'd be flattened.

From our vantage point, we could see the intruder standing perfectly still in the wheelhouse.

Brito looked worried. Where was his back-up? He peered up and down the pathway, looking for us. He talked frantically on the radio, asking for us, but we didn't answer.

Finally, he decided he couldn't wait any longer and moved in to apprehend the trespasser on his own. He stood suddenly, so suddenly that Mandy couldn't get out of the way and was knocked down. Brito was oblivious to what he had done, and we had to cover our mouths to keep from being heard. Mandy got up, unhurt, and followed him to the boat. As he stepped in, it listed about two feet to his side. Mandy followed him, not even having to step up to get over the gunwale.

We could hear Brito shout. He ordered the intruder to come down out of the wheelhouse, now, but the man didn't move.

"I'm not kidding!" Brito yelled. I clamped my hand over my mouth as tightly as I could.

When the man still didn't respond, we expected Brito to move up the ladder and bring the intruder down, but he stopped at the bottom of it, reached around behind him and grabbed Mandy by the arm. He pulled the shocked girl in front of him and handed her his nightstick, then pointed up the ladder.

Scared to death, she climbed a couple rungs, then looked back down at Brito. He urged her on, and I could almost hear him saying, "I'm right behind you."

"What's he doing?" one of my buddies whispered.

"Shhh. I don't know."

We watched in amazed delight as she reached up with the stick, which she was not licensed to carry or possess, and rapped on the intruder's leg. From our hiding places, we could hear the wooden clunks as the baton struck home. Still, the intruder did not move.

Then Jaime frantically pulled out his radio. *"We got him*

trapped in the wheelhouse, but he won't come down." He paused. *"And he's got a wooden leg."*

That was all we could take. We busted up, laughing hard and long. Brito still couldn't see us, but as we fell out of the bushes, his head snapped around.

"Hey, what the—?" He half-yelled, half-spoke, too confused to know if he was angry or concerned. Then he cautiously looked back up at the intruder who still had not moved.

He never would. He was a mannequin, dressed as a sea captain, and had been in the wheelhouse for the past fifteen years.

Realizing his error, Jaime grabbed Mandy by the waist, plucked her down from the ladder, and carried her off the boat like a small bundle of cordwood. We saw him coming, though, and by the time he reached the path, we had scattered.

We met by prearrangement at the employee break room to savor the moment. We knew Brito was mad, but also too embarrassed to do anything to us. As expected, he went straight to the station, leaving Mandy in dispatch with Wendy, and closed himself in his office.

He didn't see the briefing room chalkboard proclaiming this evening's final score: Captain Ahab 1, Jaime 0.

ELEVEN

The rest of the night passed uneventfully. I stayed busy and didn't have a chance to do any investigating, but there wasn't much left to do. Not in here, anyway. The cops had combed Solomon's Mine—it had stayed closed all day, much to John Hayes's irritation—and they had finally located the murder weapon.

I knew because Theo called me just as I was getting off. They had secured the weapon around 8 P.M. the day before. It was an iron bar loosely held by one of the static figures in a dark corner of the main cavern, not far from where I had found Everett's body. There were hairs stuck in patches of blood at one end. Everett's hair. Everett's blood.

The bar had slipped easily from the figure's fingers when touched by the cop. Theo said they had printed it, finding a few good ones. They were checking them through the state fingerprint system on a priority request and would get the results back in the afternoon.

He didn't sound too hopeful, though, and I pointed it out to them.

"The network can only check someone who's been fingerprinted," he explained. The system was not in operation when I quit, although I had heard of it. "First-timers slip through," Theo said.

"Is that the only reason you called, to tell me that?" I asked.

"Pretty much. Do you have anything to tell me?"

"No, you took me off the case, remember?"

"I didn't. The captain did."

"He didn't know I was on it."

"You know what I mean," Theo said. "Besides, I know you. You're still on it."

"Yeah, well, whatever . . . . I have nothing to report." I had a bunch of loose ends, no theories. What was there to tell him? "What about the girl?" I asked.

"The Smith girl?"

"Yeah."

"She never returned home."

"Think something's happened to her?"

"I hope not."

There was silence for a moment, then Theo said, "Well, I'll let you know if we come up with anything on the prints."

I'll bet. "Okay, Theo. Talk to you later." I pressed the button down on the receiver cradle, then placed an internal call, looking around to see if anyone was within earshot. I was alone.

A female answered. "Ride Operations."

I identified myself. "Is this Lois?"

"Yes, it is. Would you like to talk to Mr. Whelan?" Her attitude had changed. I guessed she no longer regarded me as an enemy.

"No, that's not necessary. You can help me. Did Trish come to work today?"

"No, we gave her as much time off as she needs."

"So, she hasn't called in?"

"Oh, yes, she did. This morning. That's when we told her it was okay. She's really upset about this."

"Yes, I would be, too. Well, thanks for your help, Lois."

"Is there something I can do for you?"

"If she calls, could you tell her I'd like to talk to her for a few minutes? I've got something she'd be interested in seeing."

"Well, I don't expect her to call, but I'll keep it in mind."

"Thank you."

She hung up.

I breathed a sigh of relief as I cradled the receiver. Trish was still okay, but she wasn't at home.

She was hiding. Trish knew something. Since she was wary of me, it was obvious she didn't know *who*, but I was convinced she knew *why*. So how come she hadn't gone to the police? Maybe it was just a theory, and she didn't have anything concrete to give them. Maybe she thought they'd think her idea far-fetched, implausible. Maybe she was afraid she was being watched and wouldn't make it to the cops.

Who knew the reason? The point was, I told myself, she is hiding, and I needed to find her.

I walked out toward the employee lot, passing the not-so-portable office trailers used by merchandising. Michelle Yokoyama, the vice president of merchandising, was walking toward me on the way to her trailer. She knew me by sight and smiled as she drew near.

"Good morning, ma'am," I said, nodding and returning the smile. She was a snappy dresser, always looked good. I couldn't have guessed her age if you'd paid me, and she was very pretty, with pale, clear skin, and short, dark hair.

I understood she was Nisei, second-generation Japanese-American, and her parents and grandparents had been interned at Manzanar outside Lone Pine, California, during World War II, before she was born. She was married to a Japanese businessman she had met on one of her trips to the Orient but retained her maiden name for professional reasons.

I watched her go up the steps to the trailer. Of all the vice presidents here, she was the one I'd prefer working for. Unpretentious, outgoing, she seemed the least phony of them all. But I didn't work for merchandising. I shrugged and kept walking, wondering why she had been here the night Everett was killed. It was unusual, but she had done it before.

Bert was apparently right. Married or not, she was probably meeting on the sly with someone who had career advancement potential. Not that she needed it. She was sharp in her own right.

My thought process was interrupted by a rare sighting: Jerry Opperman, the president, was actually walking around. He usually spent his entire day in his office. I had been in there once to put a packet of memos or something on his desk. His desk was not that large, but had gold-plated hardware and was hand-carved dark cherry wood with a finish so deep you could swim in it. His chair was something else. Soft burgundy leather, probably stripped off a newborn calf, with a control panel on the side for the vibra massage gizmo. It worked pretty well. I looked around to see which V.P. was escorting him, but he appeared to be alone. He walked with his head down, muttering to himself. I'd heard he was a might strange and would have been a recluse if he had enough money. I hurried ahead to make sure our paths crossed.

"Good morning, sir," I said.

"Huh? Oh, good morning." He looked up, but his eyes didn't meet mine. They were fixed on some point past my left ear.

I identified myself. "Terrible business, this Curran deal."

"What deal is that?"

"Curran, Everett Curran."

Blank stare.

"The kid who was killed in the mine ride."

"Huh? Oh, yes, that. I certainly trust it will blow over soon, though. Bad for the park's image, having people die. Not a good thing. You're with security? You've seen my new desk, then. The big one with the carved wood all over it? Had it imported."

"Yes sir, it's nice. I've seen it."

"You didn't sit in the chair, did you?"

"Well, sir, I—"

"Try it sometime. It's okay. When you're checking around, being a security guard, go ahead, sit in my chair. But don't mess with the massage controls. I have it set just like I want it. One morning I came in, and someone had monkeyed with it. Took me all morning to get it right again."

"Mr. Opperman, I'm working with the police on the Curran case, and I—"

"Oh my!" He looked at his watch. "It's almost eight! Why am I here so early?"

"You have a meeting?" I suggested.

"Yes, yes, that's it. I have a meeting. It's a Rolex." He showed me the watch. "Well, good-bye. I enjoyed talking with you. Keep up the good work."

He turned and wandered off to his office. I watched him leave and wondered, *Was he a genius or a complete idiot?* Then I remembered the midget dinosaurs and the answer became clear.

When he was out of sight, I wandered away muttering to myself.

I picked up my computer at the employee gate from Fred Billings, Ralph's replacement. Fred was a great guy and perfect for the post. He knew everyone, had been there for twenty years without holding any other position, and was completely happy.

"Whatcha got there, sonny?" He called everyone "sonny," except the females. They were "missy."

"It's a computer, Fred."

"Where's the rest of it?"

"This is all there is."

"No kidding!" He shook his head. He couldn't get over all the technological advances of the past twenty years.

"Yeah, Fred, it's a computer. Transistor radios, automobiles, liquid soap. What'll they think of next?"

He took the joshing good-naturedly as always, then greeted several incoming employees.

I had a thought. "Say, Fred, did you know Everett Curran?"

"The kid that got whacked? Yeah, I did. What an awful thing! Who knows, I may have been the last person to see him alive. 'Cept for the killer."

"Maybe so. What time did he come in?"

"'Bout five, just when I was getting off."

That validated my theory. Curran had parked his car that far out because it was the closest place available at the time. The employee lot was always full at that hour.

"Was he alone?"

"Seemed to be. He usually was."

I thought for a second. "Was he carrying anything?"

Fred pondered for a moment, then said, "Sorry, sonny. I just don't remember."

"That's okay. Thanks anyway."

"Okay, sonny."

I headed out to my van, suddenly depressed. There wasn't much I could do until I found Trish, and she could be anywhere. I felt a little helpless, wanting to crack this case, or at least find out something that would be helpful to Theo. I had the feeling the answer was at my fingertips, but I just couldn't see it.

Fingertips. I looked down at my computer and the disks I held.

"Everett, what do you have to say to me?" I wondered aloud.

TWELVE

I showered, put on a clean shirt and a pair of pants, and gathered the pile of mail that had been growing over the past few days. Advertisement, bill, bill, ad, bill, note from my doctor, bill . . . note from my doctor? What did he want?

I opened it with a table knife and pulled out the card with some apprehension, half-expecting it to tell me to call immediately. I only have a few months to live. Your test results were mixed up with a teenager's, and you're really on your last legs. You have a rare disorder found in only one percent of the population and no one has ever survived.

Phew! *It's time for your annual checkup. Please call us at your earliest convenience. We need the money and we enjoy poking around in other people's bodies.* Well, it didn't actually say that. I was reading between the lines. Maybe I should go in. I could use something to fight this rundown feeling I'd had lately.

Sleep? How gauche. Anyone could do that. I wanted a miracle drug, one that was nonaddictive, cheap, had no side effects and unlimited refills. I tossed the card with the junk mail and opened the refrigerator.

Some folks from church had suggested I get a hobby. What? I asked. Anything, they said. How about eating? They said that was more of a second vocation with me already. I enjoyed baseball. Watching it, playing it, reading about it. But that didn't seem good enough. Too seasonal. Solving murders used to be my hobby. I enjoyed it, just as I was enjoying the past few days.

Mysteries. Maybe I'd take up writing, see if I could write murder mysteries. I thought about it. Couldn't hurt to try, though I doubted I'd ever get published, even if I was any good, which I didn't know if I was or not. Well, maybe when this was over I'd give it a whirl. Right now I was hungry.

After a breakfast of corn flakes, chocolate cookies, and coffee, I spent some time in the Word. It was a struggle doing it. Picking up the Bible more, and really getting into it, was something I knew I needed to do, but being tired all the time gave me a good excuse not to. God wouldn't want me trying to study His Word when I was too tired to receive it properly, would He? I knew the answer and forced myself to crack my Bible open and read. Not anything in particular, just read. It opened to Hebrews, so I started there.

I was fascinated by the familiar passage, especially the roster of the great heroes of faith. Rahab, the harlot, made it. Her claim to fame was lying. That was tough, but the best I could figure out was that, even though her method was a sin, she was trying to exercise her faith, and God read her heart. Did that condone her motives? No. God would have worked it out without her telling the fibs. But she had real faith, and that separated her from those who spoke of faith but denied it in deed. Someone else would have given the spies up because to lie is to sin.

I felt bad for people who went to church all the time, acted like Christians, but in the final tally will be found wanting. They are so close to salvation, yet so blinded by their own efforts to achieve worthiness that they fail to realize that their responsibility is to admit that they aren't worthy, receive God's gift of grace, accept Christ as their Lord and Savior, and turn their life over to Him, letting Him control it from that point on. Too many people want to add Christ to their miserable existence but are unwilling to admit their fallenness.

I closed the book, bowed, and prayed, asking God to help me through this time of trial, to do my best to come to the bottom of this mystery, and most of all, to help me be content, to not want to chuck it all and start over again somewhere. After all, I told myself, this life is just a blip on the timeline of eternity. Our eyes should be on forever.

I checked my watch. It read 10 A.M. Time to go.

I drove to the mall where Trish and Everett's ice skating rink was located. Parking near the entrance, I grabbed a sweater from the rear of the Ford knowing it would get cold inside.

I really liked my van. It had those nifty homemade cupboards that held everything from extra clothes to pots and pans to toilet paper within arm's reach. It never hurts to be prepared.

Pushing my way through the mall door, I was met with a frigid blast of Arctic air. And that was just the mall entrance. Inside the ice rink, it was worse. I pulled the sweater on, paid for my skates—getting a ticket stub like Everett's in return—and grabbed a seat near the rink gate to put on my blades.

While tightening the laces I tried to remember how long it had been since I'd ventured out onto the ice. I recalled it was during the Winter Olympics—the year Peggy Fleming won. Or was it Sonja Henie?

I scanned the rink and the seats around it for Trish hoping, but not expecting, to see her. I knew that if she was hiding out, it was unlikely she'd be hanging around the ice rink. Still, people do strange things when they're scared and in shock. She just might retreat to a place that was important to her and Everett, especially if she thought no one knew about it. It was a shot in the dark but all I could think of right now. If I'd done what I should have in the first place, I would've taken the disks to Theo with my theories and washed my hands of it. He was certainly capable of handling the investigation from here. But some old, almost dead, ember inside me had been fanned, and a flame ignited. I had to do this, keep the flame burning.

I had begun to realize that I was losing interest in life in many respects. Homicide investigation is what made me tick. Police work in general used to do that, but after so many years of routine, I advanced to what I really wanted to be doing which was using the brain God had given me to put puzzles together, figure out the unknown, and avenge the victims of the ultimate crime one man could perpetrate upon another.

After my wife's death, the fire went out for a time, and I started looking for something else to get it going. Always searching for something to fill the void, never realizing it was God who did that; I should have rested in Him and been content to stay with the P.D.

But I didn't, and for two years now I had paid the price for my disquiet. And, barring a miracle, I saw no hope to recover what I'd lost. The P.D. wouldn't have me, and I was too old to start over with another agency. I had no choice but to do now what I should have done before and be content in whatever place I find myself.

So here I was, chasing after my demons, trying to break my own neck. I peered slowly around the rink at the skaters. There were twenty or thirty people of all ages, races, sexes, and sizes on and around the ice. None of them were Trish. I'd wait. Maybe she'd show later.

Throwing caution to the wind, I eased my way onto the ice, hoping my bones weren't too brittle. With a death grip on the rail, I set one blade on the ice, then slowly moved the other foot out. I could almost hear the theme from *Jaws.* I started to glide apprehensively and was doing okay when a Tasmanian devil wearing the guise of a six-year-old whooshed past, knocking my hand from the rail.

For a brief second my body remained upright and intact, then the horizontal line of the rail on the opposite side of the rink tilted angrily to vertical, and I slammed onto the frozen torture floor, regretting the choice I had made.

I could hear the laughing and feel the fingers pointing my direction, but when I ventured a peek, no one was paying any attention to me at all. When you're self-conscious, the whole world's your audience. I could have sworn they were laughing. Taking a quick inventory and finding nothing broken, I glanced around the rink and discovered I wasn't the only horizontal skater. Maybe life wasn't so bad after all.

I pushed myself up carefully and tried making some forward progress, keeping away from the rail and checking over my shoulder for speed demons who had no respect for their elders.

Two laps around and I was beginning to regain my sea legs. Then a young brunette cut sharply in front of me. I tried to stop to avoid her but only succeeded in losing my balance, something I had precious little of in the first place. Down I went again, this time spinning on my back with my arms and legs outstretched.

I was thinking about staying there until the ice melted and I could swim to the edge, or at least until the cold numbed the pain, when I saw the brunette looking down at me. Standing over my head, she was upside down.

"Are you an angel?" I asked.

She laughed. "No, you're not dead. I'm sorry. Let me help."

She squatted down and steadied my shoulders as I sat up, then helped me stand. Still holding my elbow she skated me over to the edge of the rink.

"Thank you," I said as I grabbed the rail. When I was steady I looked at her face.

"You're wel—"

She recognized me at the same time I recognized her. "Oh my—"

"Trish?"

She looked frantically around for an escape route.

"Wait, Trish, I'm trying to help you."

"I'll scream!"

"So will I if you don't give me a second to explain myself to you. Look, we'll go out to center ice. You know I can't do anything out there. If you want to leave, just skate away." To prove my earnestness I skated awkwardly out to the middle of the rink and waited. I looked back at her and mouthed a *please*.

Slowly she ventured out, gliding easily. She stopped short of arm's length away and folded her arms.

"Nice wig," I said.

"How did you find me? Nobody on the planet knows I'm here."

I shrugged. "Just a hunch. Everett's parents let me go through his things, and I found a ticket stub. Like this." I pulled mine out of my pocket and held it up. "I figured this place meant something special to the two of you."

The hardness fell from her face for a moment. "Everett kept the ticket stub?" she asked no one in particular. She was looking past me now, remembering, and tears welled up in her eyes. I left her to her thoughts, and after a few moments, she wiped her cheeks with her fingers. When my skates slid a little and I jerked, she snapped out of it and the hardness returned to her face. She glared at me, distrustful.

"You were in Everett's room? Just who are you? What do you want?"

"I'm with park security."

"I know. That doesn't prove anything. Someone from the park killed Everett."

"And there's a chance they're after you. That's why you ran."

She didn't answer, waiting for me to make my case.

"My name's Gil Beckman. I was the one who found him."

Her face relaxed and the tears re-formed in her eye when she thought of whom it was I had found.

"It's all in the police reports," I continued. "Lt. Theo Brown is heading the investigation. I used to work with him."

She still wasn't convinced.

"I've been to see Everett's parents. I'm positive he was killed for a reason, and you're the only one besides the killer that knows what it is. At least, that's what the killer thinks."

Her mind was still working. She didn't know what to think.

"Did you know he wrote you letters?" I asked.

"He never sent me a letter. Not one."

"No, I didn't figure he had. But he wrote them. I've got his disks." She would know about his affection for the computer.

"He thought of me as just a friend."

"I don't think so."

"Did you read the letters?" She looked angry, hurt.

"No, Trish, I didn't. I have the disks, though, and I want to give them to you. Do what you want with them. If we're going to catch this guy, I'm going to need your help. Tell me what you know."

"Is that the only way I'm going to get the disks?"

"Huh? Oh, good grief, no. I've got no use for them. They're not bait, just proof of my sincerity."

"Where are they?"

"Outside in my van."

"If I go out there, you could knock me out and stuff me in your van."

I rolled my eyes. "You're a hard sell, Trish. But that's okay. That's good. Tell you what . . . I'll meet you at the Currans'. They'll vouch for me."

"I don't know if I can."

"I understand, Trish. But you're not going to trust me any other way." I started to skate off, then stopped. "How did Beatrice turn into Trish?"

She smiled. A short, bittersweet smile but a smile nonetheless. It created dimples under her red, cold cheeks. No wonder Everett adored her.

"I was named after my grandmothers, and to avoid confusion they combined the two names and came up with Trish. My middle name is Sharon."

"Beatrice Sharon Smith." I said aloud. "Makes sense to me. See you later at the Currans', Trish." I cut a wide circle around her as I skated away. "That's where I'll be if—" I fell, looking somewhat less than graceful. She snickered in spite of herself.

"See?" I said, trying to pick myself up. "I'm harmless."

She watched me struggling with the ease of an exited dog on a waxed floor, and finally glided cautiously closer. She extended a hand to me, and I reached up to take it, looking her in the eye with as much compassion as I could muster. When I touched her hand I was surprised to find it warm, even in this deep freezer. Soft and warm, like Rachel's. For an instant I was Everett, and I knew how he must have felt about Trish. I wished I were nineteen again.

She helped me to the edge of the rink, where I tiptoed off the ice and sat down to remove my skates. As I left the place, she moved back to center ice and watched me go.

Mrs. Curran was home alone. Her husband had gone to the store and would return momentarily. She looked tired but happy to see me. She smiled and invited me in.

"Well, I found Trish," I said when pleasantries were finished.

"What did she say?"

"Nothing. She doesn't trust me. I told her to meet me here."

"Oh, it would be so nice to see her. She hasn't been by since . . . ." She trailed off.

"Yes, that would be good for both of you, I'm sure. May I use Everett's computer?"

"Please do. Have you found anything out?"

"Not yet, but I think I will soon."

I thanked her and went to Everett's room, retrieved the

keys out of the coat pocket, and sat down at the computer. I turned it on and stuck in the DOS disk. When it booted I replaced it with the word processor.

I put his X disk in the B drive and began retrieving files. As I started to read, I was puzzled. Thinking all this stuff had just been work records, I was hoping and expecting to find some tidbit of information that would incriminate one of his fellow employees in some crime or devious affair. I was surprised to see, instead, what appeared to be a proposal of some kind. Without reading further, I turned on the printer and started making hard copies of all the files.

"That may not be necessary."

The voice came from behind me. I turned to see Trish standing in the doorway, sans her wig.

"Hello, Trish. Why not?"

"I've got a copy. The whole thing. It's in my locker at the park."

"At the park?"

She nodded.

"Exactly what is it?" I asked.

"I don't know, completely. I've only seen parts of it. I think he wanted me to be surprised."

"Then why'd he give you a copy?"

"It's not really mine. It's sealed in an envelope. I was suppose to mail it to myself and then not open it, something about the postmark."

"The postmark on the sealed envelope proves that Everett had it first if someone at a later date claims it's his or her idea," I explained. "It's a common way for artists and musicians, songwriters, novelists, or what have you, to protect their work. So why didn't you mail it?"

"I was supposed to do it the day he was killed."

"When did he give it to you?"

"The day before, just before five."

"Where did that happen?"

"Here."

"Then he left for the park?"

"Yes."

"He was in his uniform, wasn't he."

"Yes, he was. How'd you know?"

I told her about the name tag, then said, "He probably figured it would be easier to get where he was going in his park uniform."

"Actually, he had just gotten off work, came home to get something and forgot to change," Trish said with an apologetic smile. "But how'd you know he went to the park?"

"What little I've seen of this plan makes me think it may be something he wanted to sell to the park. He must've had an appointment to show it to somebody. Maybe someone else found out about it and wanted the big shots at the park to think it had been their idea. They wouldn't have known about the copy you have."

"What is this that someone would kill for it?"

I pulled the paper out of the printer.

"Let's find out."

This was no small proposal. It was over one hundred fifty pages long, including artwork that Everett had scanned in. The files I had seen earlier—RIDES, COSTUMES, MERCH—weren't his work records. They were just what the names said they were.

He had designed entire rides: dark rides, thrill rides, some indoor, some outdoor, kiddie rides, each having a different theme. The whole concept was based on time travel. Each ride concentrated on a different era, or point in time, or important event in history. There were character costumes designed to go with each theme and a central character throughout the whole scheme to tie it all together: a cartoon dinosaur that walked on two legs—although it appeared to be an apatosaur—and this character was found in costumes of each event or era.

He was a cute guy with a pear-shaped body; short, skinny

legs; big feet; and an egg-shaped head with big, round, bulbous eyes on an expressive face. I could easily see the kid appeal. And the little guy had a whole family of cartoon dinosaur and human friends. It was the same character I had seen in the comic strips in Everett's files the day before.

But that was just the beginning. In the MERCH file was merchandise based on this character and the rides: stuffed dolls, a whole range of T-shirts designs, board games, figurines, toys—whatever you could think of, it was here and in great detail.

The marketing strategy Everett had developed didn't stop there. The comic strip was designed around the dinosaur and a group of kids, and was intended to be placed in daily newspapers across the country. The only direct tie-in with the park was the name of the park studio as artist/writer, but that was enough to create a national name recognition. Once the strip developed a following, every time the little dinosaur was seen people would think of the park. And the sample strips he had done were actually funny, not junior high stupid like most strips.

On top of all this, the Space Tracer game was one he developed for use on a computer. He hadn't programmed it but had laid out a vivid and detailed description of it, including all play levels and sketches of how the screens would look. It was based on a dark ride by the same name about a bounty hunter of the future.

I was amazed as the printer continued to crank out the stuff. This could revamp the entire park, give it national recognition. It might not be a Disneyland or a Knott's Berry Farm—not right away—but with this, the park would have serious potential.

Everett had also proposed an animated cartoon show, comic books, coloring books, early-reader books, and more, all centered around the friendly little dinosaur and his time machine. The whole concept was completed integrated.

Not a new idea, to be sure, but one this park needed if it

was going to be competitive. It was something that would be totally theirs on a national scale. If implemented, the park would become a true theme park for the first time, instead of a collection of over-priced European thrill rides and makeshift dark rides with poor animation and no central purpose to the whole mess. It would finally be able to be something more than a high-priced carnival. The park would have a personality, an identity.

What Everett had developed was a multimillion-dollar idea, and he had the talent to carry it out beyond mere concept to actual pre-production planning. Attendance would double or triple, plus raise millions in marketing revenues nationwide, perhaps even internationally. Dinosaurs are not strictly American. I could see this little guy standing in Red Square while wearing a fur hat, or in the middle of Tokyo wearing a kimono, or a bowler in Picadilly Circus.

There was no doubt in my mind. Everett had been killed for this idea.

I looked up at Trish who had been reading over my shoulder. The look on her face told the whole story. She knew it too. Although she had seen some of this before, she never realized it was part of a total concept until now.

When she sensed my gaze, she looked down at me. "What does this mean?" she asked, still not sure of the implications.

"What this means, Trish, is Everett had one of the most creative and forward-thinking minds in the industry. This project of his was big; and it was a sure-fire money-maker, even if only part of it was implemented. At the very least, this would be a face-lift for the park, a morale-booster for the employees, and would bring in new money, new guests, and get some good publicity."

"So, what you're saying is, someone killed Everett because of this?" She shook the pages she held.

"Not because of this, *for* this."

"I don't understand. Everett wasn't interested in money."

"Maybe not, but he couldn't help being creative. He saw

a need and came up with a solution like any loyal employee would. Besides," I leaned toward her, "he was doing it for *you.*"

This shook her, and tears welled up in her eyes. "But . . . but why would someone want to stop him?"

"They weren't trying to stop him. He was killed by someone who knew about the plan, someone who realized its potential and wanted it for themselves. That's why you're in danger. They wanted to present this to the park and take credit for it. That means they had to get rid of Everett—and whoever else knew about it."

"But I didn't know about it, not really. Not until now."

"You two were together a lot. They probably assumed you knew. I did."

"Oh." She was stunned, realizing the implication.

"Wait a minute," I said, turning in my chair. "If you didn't already have this figured out, why did you run from me yesterday?"

"I don't know," she said, staring at the papers scattered on the desk. "I was shocked, confused, upset. I didn't know why someone would want to see me. I just had a bad feeling. You know . . ."

"Woman's intuition?"

"Yeah." She acted embarrassed, as if women weren't supposed to have special intuition now that they had been liberated.

"You won't hear any argument from me," I said. "I believe in that. My wife—"

"You're married?"

"Was," I explained. "She's . . . gone." I couldn't say it, not to Trish. "She and Everett are probably talking about us right now." I tried to smile.

"I'm sorry," Trish said. Then concern rumpled her face, and she added, "Then you're in danger, too. You know about this plan."

"No one knows about me yet, though. What we have to

do now is figure out who Everett told about this, someone who wanted fame and fortune enough to kill him for it, and get to them before anything else happens."

Trish sat down and cried. It was all too much.

I made copies of the disks then put Everett's back in their hiding place and mine in my pocket. I collected all the pages of the proposal and stuffed them into a manila envelope I spotted on a shelf, then turned off the computer. I patted Trish on the shoulder, and she followed me back out into the living room. On the way, a thought came to me. The empty folder in the file cabinet, the wet tire track in the gutter, the absence of a disk file box by the computer, the pry mark on the file cabinet. Someone had definitely been here before me.

"Mrs. Curran?" She was bringing a plate of brownies out from the kitchen. Good, fattening, Christian brownies.

"Yes?" She set them down on the coffee table. I took one.

"Who was here yesterday?" I asked with a mouthful of brownie. My excitement stirred my stomach juices. "Besides Lieutenant Brown, I mean."

"Let's see. Some friends, the pastor, a couple men from the park—"

"Who were they?"

She thought. "I don't know. One of them was a man from security, I think. I really don't remember. I was so upset. They were the ones who brought me the news. The one that wasn't from security went in there and got Everett's uniforms."

I wondered. Harry Clark and Dave Whelan? Would two department heads come out for that? I thought about it. Yeah, they might. This was serious.

"Can you remember the security man?" I asked.

"Oh, let me see . . . He was short, not much hair, glasses, chubby."

"You don't remember the other man?"

"No. He didn't say much, and I was so upset. I'm sorry."

"That's all right, Mrs. Curran. May I use your phone?"

"Certainly. It's in the kitchen."

I dialed Theo's pager number from the business card he gave me, and in a few minutes, he called back.

"Theo, I've got something for you!"

"I'm glad you called. Let me be the first to tell you the good news."

"Just a second. Listen, I've got an angle on Curran's killing. I've got motive and a couple possible suspects."

"That's good, but a little late."

"Late? What do you mean, late?"

"You know, late. As in tardy, overdue, after the fact. We made an arrest not an hour ago."

"You did? Who?"

"Ride operator. Kid named Joey Duncan."

Thirteen

Joey Duncan? But—are you sure?" I sat down hard on a kitchen chair, stunned. "What do you have on him?"

"One of the prints on the murder weapon belongs to him, and he has no alibi for the evening of the murder."

"Evening?"

"Yeah. The coroner placed the time of death at around 11 P.M. And it turns out he had a disagreement with the victim a few days ago. I'm surprised you didn't hear about it."

"No one mentioned it. Apparently they didn't think it was important."

"They thought it was important enough to tell the police." Theo chuckled. "Hey, don't feel bad. You were working under a handicap. No badge.."

That hurt. "Okay Theo. Enough already. But explain to me why an argument leads to premeditated murder."

"You know motive is seldom a serious consideration. That's in the murderer's mind, may never be apparent to the rest of us unless he chooses to tell us."

"What you're saying, Theo, is Joey hasn't confessed."

"No. He emphatically denies it. But with his prints on the weapon, the argument, his record—you know what his record's like. Shoot, you're part of his record."

"Yeah, I know . . ." I was speechless. I didn't want to

believe it, but I had to admit, I'd have arrested Joey based on that evidence if I didn't know about the proposal. Theo took my silence as a sign I was done talking.

"Now, why did you call?" he asked. "You were going to tell me what you found."

"Aw, it's nothing," I said. "One question. Did you take anything from Everett Curran's room when you were in there?"

"No. Why?"

"Oh, no reason. Just curious. Well, congratulations."

I hung up and sat in the chair, my head swimming. Trish came into the kitchen a few minutes later to find me staring at the phone.

"What is it? What's the matter?"

"You know Joey Duncan?"

"Yeah. He's kind of a jerk. What about him?"

"The police arrested him for the murder." Her eyes widened, and I told her what Theo had said the evidence against him was.

"I never liked him, but I can't believe he'd do this," she said.

"My thought exactly," I admitted.

"So what does this do to our theory?"

I thought about it. "Nothing."

"Nothing?"

"Nothing. I'm going to keep checking just in case there's something wrong with Lieutenant Brown's case."

"Can I help?"

"Yeah. Stay out of sight."

"Why?"

"If the press gets a hold of Joey's arrest, the real killer—if it's not Joey—will still be looking for you. After all, when he presents Everett's proposal, he won't want anyone coming forward to dispute his claim of having created it. If you're careless, you'll play into his—" Trish was crying again. "What's the matter?"

"I don't think I can take all this!" she sobbed. Mrs. Curran heard the girl and came in. Without questioning she gathered Trish in her arms and held her. Soon they were crying together.

I patted Mrs. Curran on the shoulder. "Keep an eye on her. Maybe Mr. Curran can put her car in the garage."

Mrs. Curran looked up as if to ask, *what for?*

"Trust me, please," I said. "Keep her here, and don't leave her alone. It's important. Call her parents—"

"They're in Europe," Trish said, sniffing.

Everett's mother nodded and turned her full attention to the young woman. I felt helpless. There was nothing else I could do here, and once again, I felt like an intruder into Trish's grief.

I let myself out and drove home, then went straight to bed, having just enough time before work to get a decent amount of sleep.

But I didn't sleep. Instead, I tossed and turned for hours. I even tried praying, which usually puts me right out. For once I got all the way to *amen*, but was still wide awake. Something was bothering me—I wasn't sure just what—and I had to think it through, get it resolved. That's the way I'm made up. I don't like unresolved conflict, like getting a bill I don't owe on Saturday and having to wait until Monday to call and straighten it out.

Finally, I had to get up. I was frustrated knowing that as soon as I got to sleep I'd have to get up and go back to work, then have to spend the whole night trying to stay awake. There oughtta be a law, everything stops at midnight. Everybody—cops, burglars, donut makers, nurses—everybody sleeps for eight hours. Haven't they figured out yet that the body wasn't made for all-night duty? Let's face it, God separated the night from the day and called it good. Why'd He do that if He didn't mean for us to sleep during the dark?

I grabbed a light jacket and took off down the street at a brisk pace. I know, activity wakes you up, not puts you to sleep. But I couldn't just lay there. I berated myself for getting so involved in this deal. What was I trying to prove? That I could solve the murder better or quicker than Theo? And even if I could, why? What would it demonstrate? It wouldn't show up the P.D. They didn't get rid of me. I left them of my own free will.

But there was no stopping now, especially since Joey Duncan was in juvenile hall. Joey Duncan. Could he have done it? Was I wrong about him? It didn't make sense, not when seen in the light of his acquiescence the other day. If he had killed someone, the prospect of his losing his job would've been meaningless. He wouldn't be concerned about violating his probation.

Or would he? Juveniles were strange creatures. They do horrible things, then worry because they might be in trouble for coming home late.

No, it didn't compute. Joey would never have been able to pass off Everett's proposal as his own. Not in a million years. All they had on him was a fingerprint on the murder weapon. Okay, so that's not a minor piece of evidence. But it was the only piece. It could just as easily have been anybody else's print, any employee of the park. A reasonable explanation would create more than a reasonable doubt in the jury's mind, and without corroborating evidence, they would be required to come back with an acquittal. There had to be something else against Joey if they wanted to convict him.

Motive doesn't need to be proven in order to bring a guilty verdict, although it's nice to have. Why a killer does what he does is not a matter of law but of our morbid curiosity. Humans have a need to make sense out of everything. That's why religious cults flourish. They provide answers to the conflicts they see in the Bible, conflicts as far as our reasoning goes such as a triune God, or God's sovereignty and human responsibility. These concepts are true, to be accepted on faith, and cannot be justified in our finite minds.

We're bothered by the abstract. We need to box it up into

a pleasant little package and bring it under our dominion. That way, we are in control. The reality is that we are not in control. God is. But we have a tendency to want to swim upstream, to be the masters of our own destiny. We are bothered that Richard Speck went to the grave without ever telling why he killed those nurses. He may have had a reason, but we don't know what it was. Therefore, it was a senseless killing. I find those who are pro-choice and anti-capital punishment senseless, but that's another story.

Speck was convicted on the facts, not the reasons. Knowing someone's motives is just the frosting on the cake. There was a reason for Everett Curran's murder, but Joey Duncan didn't have one. Someone else, however, did.

I passed a small neighborhood park, one with a duck pond, and stopped to sit on a bench for awhile. The sun was still high so people were out walking their dogs, holding hands while taking a stroll, feeding the ducks. I had dealt with death for so many years that life had taken on new meaning. We truly are nothing more than a vapor, something a puff of air can dissipate. Some nut with a gun or an iron bar can take your life from you at will, make all the worry, joy, frustration, work, schooling, preparation, heartache, euphoria all void in a split second and, as often as not, feel not a twinge of remorse.

As I relaxed on the bench thinking these supremely profound thoughts, I absent-mindedly watched an older woman walking up the sidewalk, her arms laden with a grocery bag. She wasn't struggling, just carrying a few groceries home from the market as she probably did every day. I knew several senior citizens that did their shopping daily just so they could get out for a walk.

A jogger came up the sidewalk from the same direction, arms pumping, legs . . . wait a minute, this was no jogger, I told myself. He was in street clothes, black baggy pants and a black jacket too heavy for the weather. The old instinct kicked in again. I pushed myself up off the bench and began to move toward the old woman even as the running man closed in on her. If he passed her by, no sweat.

I picked a course to intersect with the two of them and broke into a trot as the man drew near. Then he reached out his arm and yanked her purse off her shoulder as he passed her, knocking her to the sidewalk, her groceries spilling. She shrieked, the strap broke, the man bolted, and people began to turn their heads to see what was going on. I shouted for someone to help her and activated the turbo.

By now I was at full bore, and the thief was twenty-five yards ahead of me, still on the sidewalk and apparently unaware of his pursuer. I didn't shout—that just makes them run faster—but tried my best to catch up. I wished I had a pair of handcuffs on me—a gun would have been okay too—but this guy looked like someone I could handle. Besides, anyone who does a snatch-and-run from old ladies is a coward.

He turned onto a residential street, and that's when he chanced a backward glance. He saw me closing in on him and, as I suspected he might, he poured it on. The advantage I had is that he had already been running some distance and was tiring. He knew it too and suddenly changed his tactic.

He hit the binders and turned abruptly to challenge me.

Don't be a hero, I told myself. Keep your distance. Find out what he's up to. I slowed down until we were separated by ten yards, then stopped. We were both breathing heavily, but I felt good, the sign of an adrenaline dump. I was ready.

"Drop the purse and you can be on your way," I said in between breaths. I had no intention of letting him go, I was buying time.

"Why don't you come get it?" he invited. Then in a swift, easy motion, he pulled a knife out of his rear pocket and flipped it open. One of those martial arts butterfly jobbers.

"You're only making it worse," I said. "First robbery, now assault with a deadly weapon. Quit while you can."

"What do you care?" he mocked. "Was she your grandma?"

"She's someone's grandma," I said, straining to listen for

an approaching siren. Nothing. People were beginning to come out of their houses. I hoped one of them had sense enough to call 9-1-1.

"It's your move, buster," I said. "Come at me, give up, or leave. You wait too long and the cops'll be here."

"Have it your way, jerk," he said, and charged, slashing the knife in the air as he bore down on me. I backpedaled, but he would be all over me in seconds. *Help, Lord!*

It was the best I could do on short notice, but theologically correct.

The man was on me now, and I could smell his breath. He stopped the slashing and thrust the knife forward to plunge it into me.

That was his mistake. I had no defense against the swipe, but this was something I could control. I brought up my right hand quickly in a clockwise arc while leaning back and caught him hard on the wrist with the back of my fist, parrying his move. At the same time, I grabbed his wrist, twisted his arm up, and drove the heel of my other hand into his exposed elbow. He shouted as it cracked and he dropped to his knees, his knife clattering onto the concrete.

With his arm still in my grasp, I pushed it into his shoulder and forced him to turn around and go down to the pavement onto his face. Maintaining pressure on the injured arm, I ordered him to put his other arm behind his back. He complied, crying and screaming.

A resident came up and retrieved the purse and the knife, which he folded and stuck in my back pocket.

"I called the cops," he said.

"Thanks."

"Need some rope?"

"Hanging's a bit extreme, don't you think?"

"No, I meant to tie him up with."

"Oh. No thanks. I can hold him until the cops get here."

"He's robbing me!" the man on the pavement shouted.

"Oh, shut up Dwayne," the resident said. "We know what

happened. We've been waiting for someone to finally get you. We're gonna have a block party over this I bet. And your lousy parents aren't invited." He turned to me. "But you are. Thanks. He's been a sliver in our behinds since he was eight."

"My pleasure," I said, hiding my amusement.

Dwayne struggled. I twisted a bit on his arm causing a little cry of pain, but he stopped moving.

The cops rolled up en masse, skidding to a stop. This time they didn't arrest me, but did what they were supposed to. I handed Mr. Bozo over to them, and they took the purse from the resident and the knife from me, then wrote down my statement and those of several other witnesses. After they finished, I walked back around the corner to the park. The old woman was seated on the bench surrounded by other cops and a paramedic who was treating her cuts and abrasions. She clutched her purse tightly as a small crowd stood around and gawked. Someone had collected her groceries.

I continued on by and went home, thanking God for protecting me and guiding me to this place. He had a reason for everything, even insomnia.

This time when I stretched out on the bed, I went to sleep. The alarm jarred me out of my slumber sooner than I wanted, however. And with the awakening came a nagging, gnawing apprehension. For the first time, I felt a sense of foreboding—that the killer was still out there, waiting for Trish, and a twinge of regret for having gotten involved in the first place, forcing myself into the lives of people who had been dealt perhaps life's severest blow—the sudden, pointless, irrevocable, violent death of a loved one.

I dressed without thinking about it, my mind filled with the image of my wife.

At work I drew the rover assignment. I could go anywhere I wanted. Actually, I asked Brito for it. I told him I'd had trouble sleeping—I didn't tell him why—and suggested that the rover spot, where I could keep moving, would be the best for me. In spite of the events of the previous evening, he agreed.

I returned immediately to Solomon's Mine. I wanted to look around, not with any particular purpose, but just to see it. The park had closed early tonight, and I didn't have to hassle with the guests at all. It's not that I don't like people; I just wanted to be alone with this thing. With Everett.

Where were you all evening, Everett? For six hours you were here, somewhere in the park. How could you be here for so long without being seen?

Being seen. He came here to be seen. He had an appointment with someone. Had he made it to the appointment? Had he seen anyone? Had Theo questioned them? Maybe he'd been confronted in the parking lot, then brought in later and killed.

No. No one knew about the proposal. How could they? It had to be someone who knew, someone he had shown it to, someone who recognized its potential. He had to have kept the appointment.

I stopped outside the mine ride and didn't go in. No, the answer wasn't in there. It was on someone's desk calendar.

I returned to the security office but took a different route through the park than I had just come, backtracking every now and then and stopping to listen, just in case Brito was spying. I didn't need his interference tonight.

When I arrived, I snuck in the back door. Brito was gone. Wendy was alone in dispatch, and she couldn't see or hear Harry Clark's office from there.

Using my master keys, I unlocked Harry's door and slowly pushed it opened. The office was dark. Clicking on my flashlight, I looked quickly around the room. Finding it empty of people, I finally let out my breath and took in another.

On the desk was his calendar. I checked it for the day in question. Nothing.

His drawers were locked. I needed to see if a copy of the

proposal was inside, just in case Everett's visit hadn't been recorded on the calendar.

Footsteps.

I clicked off my light and froze. Sweat broke out on my forehead as the steps drew nearer then receded down the hall. The heavy, lumbering steps of Jaime Brito. I opened the door cautiously, slowly, moving through the crack eyeball first, then followed by the rest of my body when I was sure I wouldn't be seen. As I pulled the door shut, it clicked, and Jaime stuck his head out of his office. Pretending not to see him, I shook the doorknob, showing it was secure. I did the same to the next door. Satisfied that I was just doing my job, Brito shrank back into his office like a turtle into his shell. I finished checking the security building to complete the illusion, then faded outside, my hands shaking.

I'd have to try Harry's office again later.

Who would be next? There were plenty of people to check, and I thought it best to progress downward, from chiefs to indians. Actually, there was little else I could do. Us indians didn't have desk calendars, much less desks to put them on. Once I had eliminated vice presidents, department heads, and their secretaries, I could move on to personal interviews with peons. Frankly, I hoped I wouldn't have to go that far. It'd take forever. I'd be up in heaven, interviewing witnesses. No suspects, though.

I decided to do it systematically, taking them in the order in which I arrived at their offices—to avoid unnecessary walking. I couldn't use an electric cart working this beat. There were too many doors and gates to go through. And I didn't want to waste time—and energy—zigzagging across the park. Oh, I could use the exercise all right, but it would take too long. And I did have regular duties to attend to, as well.

Regular duties. I was here, backstage, and figured I might as well check it and get it out of the way. I meandered through the maze of buildings and trailers, checking the shops and offices and the rear doors of the main street stores and eateries. Definite odors lingered in the air back here: rotten food and other garbage; paint; fresh bread from the bakery; hot, musty steam from the steam plant; printer's ink; gasoline . . . There was veritable palate of odors, a sampler for the proboscis.

I realized I still ached a little from my bout with Dwayne and needed the walk to work out the kinks. It had been a long time since I'd had to do that to someone. Dare I say that it felt good?

As I wandered backstage thinking about my next move, I passed Michelle Yokoyama's trailer. It was dark. Might as well start here. Glancing about to see if anyone was watching, I let myself in, keys jingling much too loud. Outside lights shone in through the windows allowing me to move about without the assistance of my flashlight. There were several small offices and items of merchandise covered every desk, shelf, table top, window sill, and much of the floor. And no two items were the same.

Many of these trinkets would make it to the park's retail shelves, hopefully to be purchased by the guests as souvenirs to fill some need to remember their day at the park. I usually rely on my credit card bill for that. Some are bought just to make Billy or Susie shut up. Most of the items in here, however, would never get this honor. They would not be approved for sale in the park by Michelle and her staff.

And yet, I had to wonder how some of the stuff they did approve ever made it past scrutiny. It wasn't all bad, of course. The main gift shop at the front of the park sold some really classy items, high-dollar stuff. But inside the park, it was a different story. Maybe Yokoyama's subordinates handled the amusement park trinket shops while she took care of the high-profile stores up front. Inside the park, the gift shacks sold some of the worst junk I had ever seen. It defies description, but if you've ever been to a theme park, you know what I'm talking about.

There was a parallel for this in other industries. Ever see a terrible movie? I mean, a truly awful stinkeroo of a movie. How is it that while they were making it someone, somewhere, didn't stop and say "Hey, wait a minute. This movie is garbage! Let's go home and start over tomorrow."

It's the same with television. Mindless babble not only gets on the tube, but everybody says it's great, including the viewers, and we treat the people that put that tripe together like geniuses, paying them scads of money to think up something just as stupid. *The Emperor's New Clothes* didn't teach us anything.

So why should merchandising be any different? Then I remembered Bert's assessment of Michelle Yokoyama's personal life. Maybe that *was* the key to success. If so, then you can have it.

And maybe Yokoyama saw Everett's idea as a way off the merry-go-round she had handcuffed herself to. Maybe she had the foresight to recognize the potential in his proposal and the need for Everett to be dispatched.

Not my personal choice for self-improvement, but desperation produces strange behavior in the natural man sometimes. But could she kill? Was she strong enough? Or did she have enough sway over someone that she could order them to take a life for her? Part of me wanted to believe the answer was *no*, but I knew better. I had seen too many people killed for flimsier reasons than a million dollars. Shoot, I'd seen people die for no reason whatsoever.

Sneaking my way through the merchandise carnage, I found Yokoyama's office in the midst of the orderly clutter with no difficulty. It was the largest, had the fanciest chair, and the most colorful fiber-optic lamp. Plus, she had a nameplate on the desk.

Heading straight for the desk calendar, I flipped the pages back to the day of the murder. There it was, plain as day. *E. Curran,* penciled in on the 5 P.M. line.

Everett had a five o'clock appointment with the vice president of merchandising to pitch his proposal, and she had apparently thought it a pretty good idea. Okay, assuming she was behind this—although the idea bothered me when I pictured her smiling, pretty face—she must have had help. Someone had to dress Everett up after probably clubbing him from behind while Yokoyama distracted him. Or vice-versa.

I sat down in her chair to think. Turning around to face the merchandise-covered credenza behind the desk, I tried to imagine her clubbing Everett, but that would be too out of character for her. So would masterminding it. I just couldn't make her guilty in my imagination. And yet, here was evidence that Everett had presented the propos—

I was startled by multiple footsteps on the stairs outside, and before I could react, the door opened. The lights came on, but I didn't move, keeping the back of my chair to them. No one spoke. They couldn't see me with the high-backed chair turned, and I couldn't see them.

Something had to be done, and I wanted to be the one on the offensive. I turned the chair around slowly, almost dramatically. Michelle Yokoyama sucked in some air and made a little involuntary noise. She stood in the doorway in front of a man who was still hidden by the darkness of the hallway. She was simultaneously frightened and surprised by my sudden appearance where she hadn't expected anyone.

"Good evening," I said, not getting up. "Your office is secure."

The man stepped around her. The first thing I saw was his gun as he moved into the light, then his arm, and finally his face. It was my turn to be frightened and surprised.

"Theo?"

Fourteen

My mind raced. If I was right about Michelle, if things were as they appeared, then I was in the soup. I'd have to be clever to talk my way out of this without letting on that I knew about Everett. But Theo? This was a possibility I hadn't considered, never in a million years, and I recoiled at the thought. But like a rush, it swept through my mind. Her desire for money, power, the opportunity to cash in on Everett's idea. Theo's position as the homicide investigator. If Theo was her accomplice, he'd need a fall guy. Had he falsified the fingerprint? And he had tried to keep me off the case. Was that Fitzgerald's idea, or Theo's? I was glad I was sitting because I got an instant headache, especially when the realization set in that my life had just become less important than my death.

"So it's you," Theo said. "I never would have figured you for it."

"Huh?" What in the world was he talking about? That's what I was about to say to him.

Theo shook his head. "I can't believe it's you. What're you doing in here?"

"Of the three of us," I said, composing myself and buying a little time, "I'm the only one that *should* be in here at this time of night."

"This isn't the man," Michelle Yokoyama said to Theo. "I know this gentleman. He's with security."

"I know him, too." Theo put his gun away. "You're sure?"

Yokoyama nodded.

"All right." He looked at me. "What *are* you doing in here?"

I had to think fast. What had they been talking about?

"Just checking on things. I needed to sit for a minute. I'm sorry, I didn't expect you to walk in. It's after midnight."

"Oh," said Michelle. "Well, I've been in very late several times during the past few weeks. We've got a big project coming up, and I can't get everything done during the day because of interruptions and salespeople I have to meet."

A big project! I thought. I said, "Why the police escort?"

"My husband and I have separated—"

"I'm sorry to hear that."

"Thank you, but it's okay. I wish it hadn't happened, but . . ."

Theo picked up the narrative. "She thinks her husband hired someone to follow her. We don't know his intentions, but she called the captain for help, and he turned it over to me since I'm already spending a great deal of time here lately. I came over tonight to check out the layout of her office and see if this guy is stalking her. Now, what are you *really* doing here?"

"I told you, Theo, checking things out." I turned to Michelle. "Ma'am, according to your calendar, you had an appointment with Everett Curran the day he was killed."

"Who?" She raised an eyebrow, her face otherwise blank.

"I thought I told you, we've closed that case," said a suddenly angry Lieutenant Brown.

"Everett Curran?" said Yokoyama. "Is that the boy who was killed?"

"Yes," I said. I pointed to her calendar. She looked over at it and saw his name above my fingernail.

"Oh, I never put the two together. I didn't realize the

dead boy was the same one I had the appointment with. I see so many people. My secretary scheduled it. That's her writing."

"You don't have to talk to him, Miss Yokoyama," Theo said. "He's just a security guard." That stung, which was Theo's intention.

"It's okay," she said to Theo. She turned back to me and moved closer. "I missed the appointment. That's when I was in with your captain, arranging this little . . . extra protection. I had forgotten about it."

"So you never saw his proposal?" I asked.

She shook her head. "I had no idea what he wanted. He said he didn't want to give it to me ahead of time." She scrunched her shoulders and held her palms up. "Sorry."

Now what? I wondered. If she had no knowledge of it, and an alibi of sorts, I could eliminate her.

Theo said, "Ma'am, would you excuse us for a minute?" He walked around the desk and grabbed my arm. "Officer Beckman was just leaving. I'll be right back."

"Okay," she said sweetly. "Nice seeing you again."

"The pleasure's mine," I replied. But further conversation wasn't possible as Theo yanked me out the door.

"Ow," I said, rubbing my compressed arm. "That's twice you guys have brutalized me."

"You're lucky I don't arrest you," Theo said through clenched teeth. "Just what do you think you're doing? The Curran case is closed. I don't want you doing any more sneaking around. Here or anywhere else."

"Okay, I guess it's time to get serious."

"I'll get serious—"

"Theo—"

"You keep your nose out of police—"

"Theo!" I shouted it. His surprise at my outburst stopped him long enough for me to sneak in two more words. "Joey's innocent!"

"What?"

"You heard me. The kid didn't do it."

"What makes you think—"

"I found Trish."

"Where?"

"What difference does that make? Would you let me explain? Just be quiet for five minutes."

He was mad but also sensible. "Go ahead. But this better be good."

"Thank you." I gave him the condensed version of Everett's million-dollar proposal and what Trish and I had discovered. "Are you sure you didn't take anything out of the kid's room?" I asked the detective.

"Yes, I'm sure. Why?"

"There's a folder missing from his file cabinet and his computer disks were taken. I found where Everett hid his backup disks. That's where I got the info on the proposal. Someone is trying to cash in on an idea he had and remove all trace of where it came from and anyone who knew about it. Including Trish."

"Is it really that big?"

"It's a complete makeover of the park. Trust me, it'd be worth millions."

"Yeah? Well, what about Joey's print? How do you explain that?"

"He works for Rides, Theo. How did *he* explain it?"

"Said he touched it a week before when he and other operators were taking an unauthorized shortcut through the mine to go on a break. He noticed it had fallen and put it back in the character's hands."

"It was loose, right? You know, not bolted in or anything?"

"Right."

"Were there other prints on it?"

"Some. Only one other print was identifiable, and it's not Duncan's."

"Whose is it?"

"Don't know yet."

"Then his story's plausible."

"Yes, but astronomically coincidental."

"Yet possible. Come on, Theo. He didn't have a motive. Not like the real killer."

"Okay, what you say makes some sense," Theo conceded. "What's your plan? Where's Trish now?"

"She's at the Currans' house."

"Okay. Let me finish up with Michelle—uh, Ms. Yokoyama. Then I'll go over and talk to Trish. But only because you're a friend."

I rubbed my arm. "I'm glad you're on my side," I said, feigning pain.

"Knock it off, you big baby," he chided. "You just do your job here and I'll see you when I come back. Mind your P's and Q's."

He re-entered Yokoyama's trailer, and I made my way out to the warehouse area where it was nice and quiet. After a few minutes, I saw his car pull out with Michelle Yokoyama sitting on the passenger side.

I wandered around the backstage area for awhile as I attempted to piece this together. There wasn't much radio traffic. All was quiet on the western front. Brito was either snoozing in his office or hiding in some bush.

Poor Jaime. I felt bad for the man, really. The guys were always playing with him, hiding from him, throwing things at him from a bridge while he walked sleepily under it, asking to meet him at the far end of the park and then changing their minds—after he had walked all the way out there.

Okay, I admit it. I did all those things, too. But Jaime really needed to grow up a little. He'd been given too much responsibility at too young an age. If he lightened up a little we'd all be more inclined to leave him alone, perhaps even help him. Maybe, when this was all over, I'd sit down over breakfast and have a talk with him.

Right now, I wanted to do some more checking. I wasn't that far from Whelan's office, although it wasn't in my area, so I made my way there. After letting myself in with my master key, I headed for his office, then pulled up short. Lois Schilling. If Whelan was in on it, so was she. I had the gut feeling that they were closer than decorum let on and figured they were partners in more ways than one. Maybe I was wrong, but I doubted it.

I took a peek at her calendar for the day in question. Somewhat surprised, I saw Everett's name penciled in. So he was going to make the rounds. Pitch it to anybody who'd listen. And after all, Whelan was his boss. That was a nice, loyal thing to do, give your boss first crack at the big idea. Only thing was, the appointment was scheduled for six o'clock.

Why didn't Whelan tell me about that when I questioned him?

There was one way to find out. I proceeded to his office and examined his calendar. Nothing. He might not have known. Lois probably made the appointment and hadn't told him about it. I guess Whelan was off the hook.

I thought about checking Everett's schedule while I was there to see who he worked with, but I didn't have the enthusiasm. I doubted I'd find any revelations. Although the idea that one of his peers might have done this was certainly possible, it wasn't plausible. Kids his age usually aren't that farsighted or visionary. They kill you for your tennis shoes or lunch money, or because you join a different street gang, but not because of a marketing idea. That involved the future and very few teens these days comprehend the concept.

I wandered out to the receiving gate. Bert was just sitting there, hands folded in his lap instead of playing his air guitar.

"What's the matter?" I asked as I got within earshot. "Break a string?"

"No, my fingers are sore." We laughed together.

"By the way," I said. "You were wrong about Yokoyama."

"In what way?"

"She wasn't fooling around. She was actually working late."

"My faith in humanity has been restored."

"Yeah, right."

"Hey, so I'm wrong." He shrugged. "What else should I think when she and Hayes are both here at all hours."

"Were they together?"

"They didn't come in together."

"When was this, Bert? Last night?"

"No, the other night when you asked me about who came in."

"You said Hayes came in after the cops showed up."

"He did. But he had only left a couple hours before that."

"Why didn't you tell me?"

"You didn't ask."

So, Hayes was here at the time of the murder. "Thanks, Bert. See you later."

"No problem."

I made my way to Hayes's office taking a long and circuitous route to avoid an encounter with Brito. Every now and then I'd key the mike switch on my radio then let up without saying anything. That opened the channel briefly, causing everyone else's radio to give off a second or two of loud static. If Brito was anywhere nearby, I'd have heard it. It was an old trick we used to keep track of him. Like putting a bell on a cat.

It worked two ways, of course. He could do it to keep track of us, unless we had our radios off. But if we did that we couldn't hear regular radio traffic and might miss a legitimate call. And the earphones didn't stay in well and were irritating, so we only used those occasionally.

Hayes's office was at the end of a hall of offices inside an area attached to the Bijou Theater, where the entertainment people made their home. I let myself in carefully. The room was dark. His windows faced an atrium that couldn't be seen from anywhere outside, so I flicked on the light switch and shut the door.

I glanced around the room. The office was neat with the

usual plaques and certificates on the wall and expensive, quality furnishings.

The massive desktop was clear—probably because Hayes didn't have any work to do—except for the usual executive gizmos: clock, phone, perpetual motion machine, huge brass paper clip, and one of those glass-globes-with-electricity-inside-that-leaps-out-at-you-when-you-touch-it thing. Whatever they're called.

In the corner was a potted palm—artificial—and on the wall was an oil painting of the park entrance, minus the trash. An aerial view of the park taken several years before, adorned the wall nearest the atrium window.

Hayes had no desk calendar.

The drawers were locked. I considered trying to jimmy them, but that would be burglary, and whatever evidence I found wouldn't be admissible—and I'd be prosecuted, without a doubt. The fact that I was in his office at all was questionable, but not illegal. I was a security guard, had a key, and was not committing a theft or any other felony. It wasn't even a trespass.

Of course, that wouldn't stop them from firing me.

I remembered Hayes's limp, lifeless handshake, and shuddered. At one time he must have been a creative man, but now he was just a figurehead. Other people did the work, he just approved or disapproved it. And Opperman—if I hadn't talked to him myself, I would never have believed it. He had to be a front for one of the owners—someone who couldn't maintain control of the park as one of ten owners, so he or she finagled Opperman into the presidency knowing that Opperman would do whatever he was told and otherwise stay hidden, emerging only every few months to remind everyone he was still here and get his picture in the paper with a gold-painted shovel.

Who was the real brains behind the park? Who really gave it direction? Apparently someone thought Curran's idea could decide that issue once and for all.

Again, it all boiled down to one thing—who knew about it? The answer: only people to whom Everett had shown it. And there weren't many of those. He didn't even show it all to Trish. He hadn't shown it to Yokoyama yet. Who else would he present it to?

Hayes, the senior vice president. The one person who could make it happen. Maybe someone else got it from Hayes, or overheard the conversation, but that wasn't likely.

If I were Hayes and Everett had given me the proposal, what would I do with it? I sat down in his chair like I had Yokoyama's and tried to become Hayes for a minute. It wasn't hard to fill his shoes, considering they were smaller than mine.

I stretched out and leaned back, tucking my feet under the desk. I accidentally kicked something, grumbled about what a nuisance it would be not to be able to stretch out under your desk, then remembered I was a good five or six inches taller than Hayes. He couldn't reach that far.

I took out my flashlight and directed it beneath the well of the desk. At the far end was a small, leather, top-opening lawyer's briefcase. I reached under and pulled it out. The initials *J.H.* were embossed in gold leaf on the side. The locking flap was only latched and opened with a metallic pop. I pulled it open and peered inside.

FIFTEEN

The briefcase was empty.

I was beginning to get discouraged. Without complete access to each person's office, desk, car, and house, I wasn't going to find what I was looking for. I set the briefcase down on the floor and pushed it under the desk with my foot, but it caught on something and tipped over. As I bent down to pick it up, the office door opened. At the same time, I spotted something on the floor that had apparently slid out of the briefcase, something I hadn't noticed when I peeked inside.

A small, blue computer disk marked with an *X*.

"What're you doing in here?" someone asked. It sounded like Brito.

I left the briefcase and disk where they were and straightened up, knocking my head on the bottom of the desk drawer. Instinctively, I grabbed the back of my head as I looked at the puzzled face of my sergeant.

"Oh, it's you," he said, actually sounding a bit relieved. "You okay?"

I didn't know. I already had a knot on the back of my melon, but there was no blood on my fingers. "Yeah, I'll be okay when my headache goes away."

"All right. Now, tell me what you're doing in John Hayes's office."

"You wouldn't believe me if I told you."

"Probably not, but let's try."

Jaime didn't move. His bulk filled the doorway. Truth or consequences time. I'd need an awfully good excuse for being in here or he'd write me up and I'd get in trouble, maybe fired. I decided to go for broke. Maybe Jaime would agree with me and help me look.

"I'm looking for evidence in the Curran killing."

Brito looked surprised, but not overly so. "I figured as much. But why here? Besides, didn't they make an arrest? Or hadn't you heard." His tone was mocking. Here I was, the big ex-cop, barking up the wrong tree. He sounded extremely satisfied. People tend to enjoy it when others stumble.

When I didn't answer immediately, Brito tried to help me out. "Perhaps you think Hayes did it."

"No, no I don't." That was a strange thing for Brito to say out of the blue. I didn't think Hayes did it, at least not directly. Hayes wasn't the type to dirty his hands. He'd get someone else to do it for him, promise him something, like a big promotion, money. ***He'd get someone who was hungry,*** I thought, ***maybe even stupid. Someone like . . . Brito.*** I looked up at Jaime, my face betraying my thoughts.

Brito held my gaze as his face slowly screwed up into an intense furrow.

"If Hayes didn't do it, who did?" He held his ground.

"I don't know," I said, although by this time I thought I did. "Maybe he hired some junky." It was a poor dodge. I stood slowly and tried to act nonchalant. Jaime moved. It was slight, but a move toward filling up my only escape route.

Jaime believed that I thought he had killed Everett, and because of his reaction, whatever doubt I harbored had been eradicated. I now knew I had to get past him or his desperation would be the end of me. Jaime had given himself away, and I think he knew it. He hadn't expected me to be in Hayes's office. Why was he here? Was he meeting Hayes?

I took a step toward the door, but Jaime filled the hole. He turned as Hayes walked in. It was now or never.

"What's going on here, Jaime?" Hayes asked.

"Mr. Hayes!" I shouted, "you're under arrest for the murder of Everett Curran!"

It was a stupid thing to say, but I didn't have time to think of anything better. I needed to distract them, give myself an edge.

"What are you talking—?" He looked at Brito.

"Hey, I didn't tell him!" Brito interrupted.

"You just did, you idiot!"

"And you just confirmed it, Mr. Hayes," I added.

"You've got nothing on us." Hayes's face was reddening, giving himself away. Just as water rises in a well when the source is tapped, fear bordering on panic was rising in Hayes. Something would happen soon if I didn't take the initiative, and I doubted I would be waltzing out of here singing *Zip-A-Dee-Doo-Dah*.

Jaime's apprehension was growing too. He frantically looked back and forth between Hayes and me. There was no time like the present. When his head was turned away from me, I grabbed the electric glass globe and threw it at his head. He winced and shut his eyes as the globe struck his forehead opening a nasty cut, but the glass didn't break. I was instantly on the move and put all my weight into Brito's midsection, knocking him back a step or two. He tripped and fell backward, unable to keep his balance. I reacted to his mass by bouncing the other way into the potted palm.

As I went down I caught a fleeting glimpse of John Hayes's Italian shoes and remembered my sketch. Before Hayes could react I lunged at him, grabbed his leg, and jerked it out from under him. He crashed to the floor, and I crawled over him into the hallway.

As I stumbled down the corridor, I heard Jaime rumbling after me. Was he growling?

I hit the outside door running and ducked down a back

alley that ran around a portion of the perimeter railroad. Even at twice his age I knew I could outrun Jaime, but what then? I had my radio but couldn't slow down to get it out, not just yet. I needed to find myself some breathing room.

Not knowing how good Jaime was with a gun, I didn't move in a straight line, which slowed me somewhat. I ducked between the corner of the dino ride and an outbuilding, stopping in a shadow. I grabbed my radio, then thought better of it. Jaime would hear me, and Hayes was also known to carry a radio so he could keep tabs on everything. I needed to get to a phone.

I was alone. No one else knew anything. No one would be coming to help, and who would believe me anyway?

Whelan's office was just across the road. I peeked out for some sign of Brito. Nothing. I couldn't have lost him this quickly. He'd still be close enough that I should be able to hear him. I listened again. Still no sound.

I took a chance. Pushing off from the wall I charged across open ground, keeping low. I was halfway across when Jaime tore out from some nearby bushes and bore down on me. He knew the bushes like the back of his hand.

Surprised, I yelped involuntarily but didn't slow down. He lunged at me, his large hand grabbing at my arm. I pulled free, swung blindly at him and hit something solid, then stumbled, but was able to keep running as Brito lost his balance.

I glanced over my shoulder and saw Brito hit the ground and roll, but his momentum brought him right back up on his feet. He was more agile than I realized, and I groaned.

"Okay, Lord, I need you now," I said out loud through gasps for breath. My eye caught a directional arrow used to guide park guests to the wilderness ride where guests sit in a hollowed out log and float down a chute through the backwoods country that is populated by cutesy animated woodland creatures and demented-looking elves. Normally not a believer in visions, I nonetheless followed the arrow.

I cut around a trash bin, jumped a rail, and leaped over the chute at the loading dock. The water had been drained into the underground reservoir for the night, and the chute was dry except for small puddles here and there. Fiberglass logs were lined up at the dock. Bottomed out in their dry bed, they were fairly unstable because of the curvature of their bottoms.

Down a short slope from the dock, the logs would be hauled by chain up a long, steep, incline—similar to the beginning of a roller coaster. Once at the top, the easy float down would begin, ending in a sharp free fall down a forty-five degree waterfall into a splash pool.

I climbed the narrow stairs at the side of the first incline as Jaime made it to the loading dock. He hadn't drawn his gun. I wondered why not. Perhaps he was so mad he hadn't thought about it, or didn't want someone hearing it and calling the cops. Or maybe he just wasn't desperate enough yet, confident he could take care of me by himself.

What had Hayes promised him? What do you give someone in exchange for murder? Money? Position? Both? I scrambled to the top of the incline and ran out to the other side of the shed that housed the first animated scene. Men in a sawmill stood on raised platforms on both sides of the log chute sawing the same logs day after day, year after year.

I stopped for a moment to catch my breath. My lungs screamed. Although not in bad shape, I wasn't use to this. But Jaime was not quitting. Blinded by rage and his own fear, he lumbered up the ramp, his eyes boring into me with an intensity I had never seen in him.

Already his shirt was soaked, as it had been the night of the murder, I realized. I left the chute and cut across the gunite toward a service door invisible to the public in a cleft in the rock. It was not locked—there was no need due to its location—and I threw it open.

Another indoor scene swallowed me. I was instantly transported to a mythical, magical forest populated by gnomes and deer. All happiness and warmth. An employee trail led me behind all the scenery, and in the near pitch-black, everything looked fairly realistic. That's why all these rides were dark. They couldn't stand the scrutiny they would get in the light. This would have been a good place for a scriptural application had the door not yielded to Brito's shoulder.

I kept running, ignoring the scenery, and went through another door. I couldn't hide. My breathing was too hard and would give me away. I continued down a short passageway and through a third door which opened to reveal a staircase. I took them, more or less gliding by my hands on the shining rails, my feet in the air. Both of my palms were burned from the friction, but that was offset by the extra seconds I gained.

The stairs emptied into a workroom. I closed the door behind me and locked it, buying a few seconds. I knew Jaime had keys, but he was agitated, and it would take him a little extra time to find the right one and get it in—I hoped.

I grabbed the receiver of the workroom phone and punched in the extension for the receiving gate. It rang twice—taking an eternity to do so—before Bert answered.

"It's your dime."

"Listen, has John Hayes driven out?"

"No. What's going on? You sound terrible."

"Shut up and listen, this is serious. Whatever you do, don't let Hayes out. He had Curran killed. Jaime did it—"

"Are you nuts?"

"No! Would you listen? Lieutenant Brown should be coming back in pretty soon."

"The blue Ford?"

"Yeah, that's him. Tell him to hold Hayes, and to look under Hayes's desk. And call Wendy now, have her phone the cops."

"What's that pounding?"

"That's Jaime trying to kill me. Don't send any of the guys in here. I don't want anyone hurt."

I hung up just as the knob started to turn. Seeing a fire extinguisher on the wall, I grabbed it and expelled it at the door just as it burst open. The chemical hit Jaime full in the face, and he fell back. I didn't wait around to see what other effect it had on him. I dropped the canister and fled in the opposite direction. A door slowed me before I broke out on the employee side of the loading dock.

I ran across the unstable logs, but I'm light enough on my feet that I didn't fall. A jump down three steps, two leaps over railings, and I was on my way.

Jaime was not far behind. Breathing hard and looking like the loser in a flour fight, he kept pace with me. I had to keep him off me long enough for the cops to get here.

Solomon's Mine loomed ahead of me. I ran down the entry ramp, through a short cave, and onto the loading dock. Picking my way carefully down the track, trying not to step on the greasy rail, I entered the mine.

It was so pitch-black in here that I had to click on my flashlight. I ducked inside the first sneak-in I came to and turned the flashlight off. The night lights they left on in the workroom were sufficient. I was met with a latticework of ladders and staircases that gave the workers access to just about every section of the multilevel mine from this one central room.

I could hear Jaime inside the tunnel. I moved as quietly as I could to a dark shadow under a staircase and waited, watching the sneak-in I had come through. I was surprised when Jaime came suddenly down the stairs I was hiding under. The cut on his forehead wasn't as bad as it seemed at first. It was just oozing now, and there wasn't much blood on his shirt.

I froze. He hadn't seen me. He stopped, looked around the room, then retreated back into the tunnel. I moved quickly across the room, passing the employee break room. When I glanced inside on my way by, I remembered the candy wrappers on the table and realized where Everett had been those hours before he was killed. I wondered if Theo'd had that room fingerprinted.

But I couldn't worry about that now. I dodged through another sneak-in and found myself in the bottom of the main cavern, not far from where I found Everett. I stopped and listened.

Jaime's heavy footfalls were above me. The beam from his flashlight moved swiftly around, searching. I tiptoed back down the sneak-in and up a staircase, then into the tunnel. I walked along the track and saw Jaime in the main hole where I had just been. Suddenly I tripped, and his flashlight found me.

He yelled and lumbered towards the nearest access door. I raced along the tunnel, into a sneak-in, and down the stairs—just as Jaime was starting up. I backed up as he saw me, back into the sneak-in, and pressed myself against the wall in the darkness. He ran past me as I blended into a crevice in the gunite. I broke and ran down the stairs, through the workroom, and through a door onto the tracks. I ran up a sharp incline and found myself in a magnificent cavern filled with stalactites and stalagmites. The colors were intense, at least those captured by my flashlight. A small rock I kicked fell into an underground lake below me.

The door at the bottom of the incline opened and Jaime came through. I climbed down under the trestle and hung below him as he slowly walked above me, looking in the stalagmites and stalactites. Not finding me, he continued down the tracks and out of the cavern.

I climbed back on top of the trestle, then retreated down the incline, ventured through another door, and found myself on the loading dock. Jaime popped out from one of several tunnels on an upper level, saw me, and picked up the chase. With Jaime in close pursuit, I ran down the ramp and back out onto the midway.

Why didn't I just take Brito out? Frankly, I didn't know if I could. This cat-and-mouse game was wearing me out, but I had the feeling he wouldn't give up easily, and I'd have to take him out all the way. After all, he was fighting for his life.

Besides, he had a gun, and I didn't. So I ran.

What area did I know better than Brito? He had been here longer. But then, he hadn't known about Captain Ahab. I was here when they built the dino ride, walked through it every night while it was under construction. I knew every curve in the track—I could walk it blindfolded—and every sneak-in and hiding place.

I ran under the entrance arch and up the ramp, then jumped the rail onto the loading ramp and disappeared into the ride. Bypassing the first scene—an archeologist's lab—I cut behind a false front and stepped into the Ice Age.

A prehistoric man—who would have looked more natural in a department store window—ignored me as he stood motionless, searching in the silence for an animal to kill. If I'd had the time, I would have pointed out a couple midget mastodons in the next room.

It was funny how the humanoid was actual size while everything else was greatly scaled down. This place needed Curran's genius. Noises on the loading dock reminded me that I had more important things to think about, and I pressed on, going further back in time with each step.

Was that a siren? It was hard to tell in here. I followed the track through the tar pits, past the two-by-three foot aurora borealis, and into a dark tunnel occupied by large spiders and other bugs.

I was surprised by the unexpected appearance directly behind me of the wraith-like Jaime. His hand was reaching for his gun. His patience had evidently reached its limit.

Time to play hardball.

I turned and grabbed the only solid object I had—my radio. I turned it on as I keyed the mike and shouted "Dino ride!" before throwing it at Jaime. It struck him in the shoulder, and his gun clattered to the floor.

As he bent down to retrieve it, I ran up a short incline in the track, then slid back down the other side, coming to rest a few feet from a gigantic four-foot-long dimetrodon. Scary, scary.

Regaining my feet, I scampered through a sneak-in, popping out into the main room where the stegosaur, tyrannosaur, and apatosaur roamed. The rocks in here were made from polyfoam. The animated figures were soft to the touch and not really suitable for daily use. Their skin had cracked at the folds, and many had stopped working altogether. It was all the same now, though, with the power off. The T. Rex was no more frightening than a cocker spaniel.

Brito, on the other hand, was a different story. I definitely heard sirens now and knew they would be converging on the dino ride any moment. It was time to hide.

From a place I found, I peeked through a crack in the scenery and saw Brito walking cautiously into the room, his gun resting comfortably and menacingly in his hand. It turned in conjunction with his head as he looked around for some sign of me. I took my breaths as easily as I could. The pain in my chest intensified. My head still ached from the bump I got under Hayes's desk.

Oblivious to the approaching sirens, Jaime moved slowly through the room, knowing I was in there. He was a man on a mission. He passed me unknowingly. I considered jumping out and trying to disarm him. Just as I ruled it out, a blue suit popped into the room. He saw Jaime, but, knowing him to be an armed guard, the cop did not sense the danger.

Brito did, though, and began to raise his gun toward my would-be savior. There was no question now, no more time for thought or restraint. Or fear. I stepped out of the crevice, leapt on him, and grabbed his revolver around the cylinder so it couldn't turn, and the gun couldn't be fired. But I had to hold on. With my other hand I hit him solidly in the side of the neck then gave him a leg sweep, and down he went.

As he landed, stunned by his own weight, I pounced on him, making sure he had no wind in his sails. While he fought to take a breath, I wrenched the gun out of his hand. The cop-—who had been transfixed and confused by a fight between two security guards—-had pulled his gun but wasn't sure who to shoot. It was my favorite rookie. I called him by name to snap him out of it.

"Collins! This is the killer! Give me your cuffs!"

He recognized me, putting it together finally, and came to us in a hurry. I handed him the pistol as he passed me his handcuffs. Jaime was prostrate on the track on his stomach, his hands secured behind him. I watched him for a second to see what he would do and was surprised that he did nothing. Then I realized he was sobbing. He looked up at me, more hurt than angry, tears and sweat rolling down his cheeks, mixing with the ooze from his forehead wound.

"I was going to be security chief," he spat at me. "And you ruined it." Collins grabbed him to roll him over and sit him up. Brito didn't resist, his attention riveted on me, and Collins managed to stand him up with some difficulty. He led my former supervisor out of the ride and down the ramp as I forced myself to hold my peace, to not hate Jaime for taking an innocent life to get a promotion.

I stood in the shadow of the apatosaur, my mind and my body both overwhelmed and exhausted. The long neck of the beast hung over me like a tree limb, it's animation suspended until the park opened in the morning. The unblinking eye stared at me, and its foliage-eating mouth seemed locked in a grin.

"What?" I asked.

When it didn't answer, I moved slowly out to the end of the ride then out onto the loading dock. As I walked achingly down the ramp to the midway, I saw two people headed up toward me. Theo and Trish.

Trish ran ahead of the lieutenant and met me halfway up the ramp, wrapping her arms tightly around me.

"You did it," she said. I was too tired to answer, and when I patted her on the shoulder she started to sob. "Why?" she asked. "Why?"

I didn't know. Not yet. What could I say that hadn't already been said? My own eyes filled, partly from relief and partly in sympathy for her. It was over, but it would never be over.

Theo stepped up and handed her a clean handkerchief as she broke from me. While she stepped aside to take care of herself, Theo filled me in.

"I heard the call when I was at the Currans', talking to Trish. She detailed the plan for me. Quite a deal. I brought her with me. Couldn't keep her away, actually. She was worried about you."

"Why?" I asked. "There's no ice here."

Theo was puzzled by that one, but Trish smiled. Theo shrugged and continued.

"Hayes was headed out when I turned into the driveway. The guard saw us both, and when he noticed that Hayes wasn't slowing, he tossed his stool onto the windshield. Hayes lost it and hit the fence, and Trish told me who he was." Theo stopped for a moment in case I had a question, but I was too busy trying to breathe. He went on.

"The missing file folder was on the seat next to him, along with a finished copy of the proposal, the one Curran had given him. Curran's name had already been whited-out." Theo pulled something out of his pocket. It was the blue floppy disk from under Hayes's desk. Theo smiled.

"Hayes started blathering as we loaded him into the ambulance. Everett came to him with the proposal. Hayes recognized its value to him if he could claim credit for it. He knew he could bribe Brito into doing the deed." Theo shrugged. "He said he hadn't meant for it to happen here, but Brito got excited and jumped the gun. That's all we got out of him before they took him off. I'll talk to him in the jail ward of the hospital tomorrow. His injuries aren't serious."

"What about Joey?"

"I radioed in to have him released. He should be on his way home soon."

I leaned against the rail, my chest and legs still punishing me for the treatment I gave them.

"I owe you one," Theo admitted quietly.

I waved him off.

"We're even," I said. "I had to do something to regain your stature in the department for you." I grinned and started down the ramp, but my legs buckled.

"Here, let me take you home," Theo said, helping me to the rail. "You can give me your statement tomorrow after you get some sleep."

"No, I'm okay. I'll meet you at the station in a little bit. Could you see that Trish gets back to the Currans' house? And tell them I appreciate their help."

"You got it . . . friend." He grinned and slapped me on the shoulder.

As I clung to the rail, I watched them walk off. Trish turned her head back toward me once, smiled a little, and waved. I waved back.

When I had regained enough strength, I walked out past a blubbering Jaime who sat in the back of the rookie's black and white while the cop took down some custodians' statements. Apparently they had witnessed some of the chase. Collins saw me and I met his eyes, then smiled and gave him a thumbs up. He grinned and nodded and went back to business.

I took the long way so I could pass by the receiving gate. Bert was still there, watching the cops do their work on Hayes's car. He saw me and beamed.

"Did you hear? Was I great, or what?"

I had to smile. "Yeah, Bert, you were great." I shook his hand. "You were better than great. Thanks."

"You look terrible," he pointed out.

"Thank you." Once again I took that as a compliment. I felt dead, and terrible is better than dead. Isn't it?

A car hit the driveway from the street and screeched to a halt beside the booth. It was Harry Clark. Wendy had apparently summoned him right after calling the cops.

"What happened to you?" he asked, looking at my torn and dirty uniform.

"Nothing." I said as I took off my badge and stuck it in his dashboard. "Nothing that a new job won't fix."

I walked away. Harry stared at me, not knowing what had happened. I hated the park and its poor management that allowed something like this to happen by promoting the unqualified while ignoring the worthy.

But I stopped myself before reaching his bumper. Was I doing it again? Was I making another rash decision based on how I felt instead of seeking the Lord's will?

I turned and walked back to Harry's open window, reached in and picked up the badge.

"Just kidding," I said. "I'll be back in the morning. The cops can fill you in."

I pinned the badge back on my torn shirt and walked confidently, almost proudly, to the yellow behemoth.

SIXTEEN

Two days later Everett Curran was laid to rest. I've always hated funerals, but this was one I needed to attend. Everett and I'd had a short, but intense, relationship, and I wanted to say a proper farewell. I stayed in the back of the church, not seeing his family or Trish who were hidden in a room off to the side, and left as soon as the service was over.

I walked silently to my van and stood next to it, fingering the bandages on my face and arms as I waited for the procession to the cemetery to pass. I had decided to forego that part of it, leaving the graveside service to his parents and close friends. I was absentmindedly watching the last car leave the church when someone came around toward me from the back of my van. Theo. I gave him a single nod.

"Morning, Theo."

"Morning, Gil."

"So, what's new?"

"Hayes confessed. At least, in his own special way. He tried to blame Brito for it all saying he only meant to buy the proposal, give the kid a few thousand dollars for his work, and then was going to fire him."

"Everett was naive, but not that naive," I said.

"Hayes found that out. When they were in the mine break

room talking about Everett's plans for the park, they got into a rather heated discussion."

"I doubt that. Everett wouldn't get into a heated discussion with anyone."

"My thoughts exactly, but that's Hayes's story. He said Everett jumped at him, and Brito clubbed him to protect Hayes."

"What did Brito say?"

"That he went along just to make sure Hayes was okay, that Hayes was his meal ticket and he wanted in on the action. He claims he was willing to push Everett around a little bit, but Hayes wanted him dead and all the loose ends tied up. Brito was afraid of Hayes, so he did it."

"Sounds like a truer story."

Theo nodded. "The coffee cup in the mine break room—it had Hayes's prints on it. And we served a search warrant on his house and brought in all his shoes. They were all the same basic style and shape, and two pairs, both new, matched the cast. They were identical except for color. So we looked a little closer: one shoe had a tiny bit of Everett's dried blood in the welt. He had wiped them off, but too hastily. We also found the missing stuff from the boy's room . . . the file folders and the computer gizmos."

He paused. "Oh, and I found out something else. Hayes knew nothing about Trish, didn't have an inkling."

I closed my eyes and dropped my head, shaking it slightly. All that worry and loss of sleep, completely unnecessary.

"Don't feel bad," Theo said, sensing my mood and my thoughts. "Because of your concern for Trish's safety, you were driven to find the solution. That's good detective work."

I stared at my shoes. "Well, I'm glad that's over with." I looked up and exhaled. "I've got to admit, it was fun. I miss the P.D., Theo. You don't know how much."

"Yeah, I bet you do. That reminds me, I've got a message for you from Captain Fitzgerald."

"The department wants me to come back, right?"

Theo smiled wryly. "No. What makes you say that?"

"Oh. Well, I just thought . . ."

"Sorry, buddy, but nothing's changed. You're still persona non grata there, at least as long as 'Don't Call Me Bill' is alive."

"Hope springs eternal," I muttered. "What did he want?"

"He said to tell you to mind your own business next time."

I laughed. It was the only reasonable response.

"Hey, you're better off," Theo suggested.

"Huh?"

"Look what I have to put up with."

"Yeah, but the pay's better."

"Not necessarily."

"What do you mean by that?"

"You're in private industry, Gil. The sky's the limit."

I waved him off. "Aw, it doesn't matter anyway. I'll stay on graveyard, keep doing what I'm doing. It'll be okay. Besides, I think I'm where God wants me."

"You said that when you quit the P.D."

"True. But before, it was an excuse to follow my own plan. This time it means I'm going to stay put, see what He has in store for me."

"Let me know how it turns out."

"Don't be such a stranger," I challenged. "Maybe I'm not a cop, but I'm still your friend. And I'm still just around the corner."

Theo smiled and held out his hand. "You're right, partner. I apologize for the grudge I've been carrying."

I took his hand. "Accepted. And I'm sorry for giving you a reason to have one in the first place."

He slapped me on the shoulder. "See you soon, Gil."

"Soon, Theo."

I watched him walk away, then drive off. As I turned to climb into my behemoth, a black Mercedes pulled up alongside me. I watched with mild curiosity as the tinted driver's window lowered with an electric hum.

"Mr. Beckman," Michelle Yokoyama said, the smile on her face genuine. "Do you have a few minutes?"

"Sure."

"Please, get in."

I looked at her for a second, then shrugged and walked around to the passenger side of her car. As I eased into the tan leather seat, I realized it was the first time I had been in a Mercedes. Not bad.

"Sorry to see you again under these circumstances," she said.

"It must be hard for you, too," I acknowledged.

"Yes. It was quite a shock. Have you heard? I'm the new senior vice president."

"Great! Congratulations," I offered. "You deserve it."

"Thank you. Listen, I'd, uh, like to talk to you sometime soon," she said. "At length. Are you free tomorrow afternoon?"

"Tomorrow's Sunday. I've got Someone I have to spend the day with. Monday is the soonest I can do it. What's this all about?"

"I want you to go over Everett's proposal with me. You're the most familiar with it. I think it deserves some serious consideration. If we go for it, the boy's family will receive Everett's share of the benefit. I anticipate a substantial royalty share. I had Lieutenant Brown speak to them yesterday. They were very excited about you being involved."

"I'm not very creative," I said.

"I don't believe that. I think if we put our heads together, we could make a good team."

"Won't that look kind of funny? I'm just a security guard."

"Well, not if you don't want to be. I'm going to take you on loan for awhile, if you're amenable. A man of your experience shouldn't be shaking doors all night long. And it will mean a substantial raise. This is going to be an important project to the park, and because it's going to be costly, implementation is going to be spread out over several years to allow the increased revenue we anticipate to catch up to our outlay. Actually, you might never have to go back to being a security officer."

"Huh?" Not a very intelligent response, but she had caught me off guard. I recovered quickly, though. "Uh, I think I'm going to need an assistant."

"Have anybody in mind?"

"Well, there's one other person who knows about Everett's plan. His girlfriend, Trish Smith. She works in rides."

"Done," Michelle concluded. "We'll iron out the details Monday."

She offered her hand to close the deal, and I took it. I got out of the car, and she smiled and waved, then drove off. For a long time I stood there in disbelief, stunned. My head began to spin.

In fact, it was still spinning later that evening as I stood in Sally's living room pinning her corsage on with shaking hands.